The
Clintons
of
Arkansas

The
Clintons
of
Arkansas

An Introduction by Those
Who Know Them Best

Compiled and Edited by
Ernest Dumas

The University of Arkansas Press
Fayetteville 1993

97 96 95 94 93   5 4 3 2 1

Designed by John Coghlan

The paper used in this publication meets the minimum requirements of the
American National Standard for Permanence of Paper for Printed Library
Materials Z39.48-1984. ⊚

Library of Congress Cataloging-in-Publication Data

The Clintons of Arkansas : an introduction by those who know them best /
    compiled and edited by Ernest Dumas.
        p.   cm.
    ISBN 1-55728-288-9
    1. Clinton, Bill, 1946–   . 2. Clinton, Hillary. 3. Presidents—United
States—Biography. 4. Presidents—United States—Wives—Biography.
I. Dumas, Ernest, 1937–   .
E886.C58   1993
973.929'092—dc20   93-12648
    [B]   CIP

Acknowledgments

This volume could not have been finished without the cooperation and support of others, only a few of whom I acknowledge here. First, obviously, are the contributors of the articles, who endured the repeated importuning of the editor. Several of them deserve gratitude also for supplying photographs. Polly O'Brien of St. Louis, who worked in Clinton's first gubernatorial administration, and Donna Wingfield of Prescott, Arkansas, a friend from kindergarten days, supplied photographs, as did Joe Purvis, Tom Campbell, Steve Smith, Ann Henry, and Diane Blair. I am indebted to Pat Harris, a reporter for the *Hope Star,* who provided tapes of interviews with neighbors and friends of Clinton from his childhood at Hope. I want to thank George Fisher for generously, as always, allowing his cartoons to be used, and the *Arkansas Democrat-Gazette,* the owner of the *Arkansas Gazette,* where most of Fisher's cartoons were first published. The Arkansas Writers Project and Paul Greenberg readily gave permission for the republication of Greenberg's column. Acknowledgments would not be complete without mentioning Debbie Bowen, a splendid editor at the University of Arkansas Press, and others at the Press who worked on this volume. Finally, I want to thank Elaine Dumas, whose encouragement and patience are always unflagging.

Contents

Contributors

Phyllis Anderson was an administrative assistant to Governor Bill Clinton and is the author of a book about his first term as governor. She lives in Little Rock.

Woody Bassett, a lawyer who lives in Fayetteville, Arkansas, was a former law student of Bill Clinton's and Hillary Rodham's.

Diane Blair, Bill's and Hillary's longtime friend, is professor of political science at the University of Arkansas and the author of a book about Arkansas government and politics and a book about Hattie W. Caraway of Arkansas, the first woman elected to the United States Senate.

Tom Campbell, who lives in Orange, California, was Bill Clinton's roommate for four years at Georgetown University.

William T. Coleman III, a lawyer who lives in Detroit, was a classmate of Bill Clinton's and Hillary Rodham's at Yale University and shared a house with Clinton in New Haven, Connecticut.

Dale Drake was Bill Clinton's neighbor in Hope.

Ernest Dumas, the editor, teaches journalism at the University of Central Arkansas in Conway and writes a column for the *Arkansas Times.* He was a reporter and editorial writer for the *Arkansas Gazette.*

George Fisher was the chief editorial cartoonist for the *Arkansas Gazette* from 1976 until the paper's demise in 1991. He owns a commercial graphics firm in Little Rock.

Mike Gauldin, a former editorial cartoonist, was press secretary to Governor Clinton from 1987 through 1992 and now is communications director at the United States Department of Energy.

Paul Greenberg is editor of the editorial page of the *Arkansas Democrat-Gazette* in Little Rock and former editorial-page editor of the *Pine Bluff* (Ark.) *Commercial.* His columns are nationally syndicated.

Bob Lancaster is a freelance writer who lives in Sheridan, Arkansas. He is a columnist for the *Arkansas Times* and is the author of several books of fiction and nonfiction.

Rudy Moore, Jr., is a lawyer and municipal judge in Fayetteville. He managed Clinton's first campaign for governor and later was his chief of staff.

Margaret Polk lives in Hope.

Joseph Purvis, a kindergarten classmate of Clinton's and later a lawyer in the office of Attorney General Clinton, practices law in Little Rock and is leader of a rock band, Little Joe and the BKs.

Roy Reed, a former reporter for the *Arkansas Gazette* and *The New York Times,* is professor of journalism at the University of Arkansas and a freelance writer. He lives in Hogeye, Arkansas.

Dr. Bobby Roberts is director of the Central Arkansas Library System in Little Rock. He was a legislative assistant and correctional advisor to Governor Clinton.

Paul Root lives in Arkadelphia, Arkansas, where he is chairman of the Department of Education at Ouachita Baptist University. He was a high-school social-studies teacher of Clinton's in Hot Springs.

James L. "Skip" Rutherford, a political advisor to Clinton, was chairman of the Arkansas Democratic party in the 1980s. He was a deputy director of Clinton's presidential campaign. He lives in Little Rock.

Brack Schenk lives in Hope.

Stephen A. Smith is chairman of the communications department at the University of Arkansas and was at one time a member of the Arkansas House of Representatives. He was a friend, political advisor, and administrative assistant to Clinton in the early years as attorney general and governor. He lives in Fayetteville.

Carolyn Staley, a high-school friend of Clinton's in Hot Springs, is a former opera singer. She lives in Little Rock and heads the state program on adult literacy.

George Wright, Jr., an old friend of Clinton's, was a kindergarten classmate and later an official in Clinton's administration as governor. He still lives in Hope.

Carl Whillock, former president of Arkansas State University, was an early friend and political advisor of Clinton's. He is president and chief executive officer of the Arkansas Electric Cooperatives Corporation and lives in Little Rock.

Introduction

Had he waited until the day of his inauguration as president to resign as governor of Arkansas, William Jefferson Clinton would have served longer than any other governor in the state's history, a week more than twelve years. Every four years for most of the previous century and a half, ambitious men had wearied of the frustrations of the office or else the voters had grown sick of them. Usually, the politician and the voters arrived mutually at that decisive moment. Only two other governors ever kept the voters' allegiance longer than four years. One was Jeff Davis, a bellicose populist at the turn of the century who satisfied those whom he called his people, "the wool-hat brigade, the horny-handed, sunburned sons of toil, the men that pull the bellrope over the mule," by roaring against their twin enemies—the unlikeliest groups ever yoked together, big corporations and "the negroes." The other was Orval Eugene Faubus, who briefly defied the United States government in defense of racial segregation during his second term in 1957 and parlayed it into eight more years in office.

The shibboleths of bigotry were not the source of Clinton's magic with voters. He was the undemagogue. He could hardly have done more than he did to alienate the people out at the forks of the creek. "For as long as I can remember," he declaimed in his first inaugural address, "I have believed passionately in the cause of equal opportunity, and I will do what I can to advance it." He reached out to the 15 percent of the Arkansas people who were African Americans and put more of them in public offices and government jobs than did all his predecessors combined. Nowhere were taxes more loathed than in Arkansas, which had the lowest per-capita tax burden in the country, but he raised taxes every two years that he was in office. He raised the hopes of every constituency in the state, and then disappointed most of them. Led to expect miracles, they were dismayed at simple good works. In seven statewide elections, nevertheless, Clinton won six, all by landslides.

How he did it is not in doubt. After all, the formula made him president. Few Americans ever had the exterior gifts of the politician in such abundance. Bill Clinton was handsome, loquacious, and tireless. He always exhibited a boundless optimism. He met people with grace and facility, and a prodigious memory never let him forget them. He had what seemed to be a compulsive need to meet people, to know them, to like them, to have them like him. These are the instincts of a calculating politician, but the evidence of essays in this book suggests that they long preceded Clinton's political impulses. Bill Clinton's is a case where a man's deepest human instinct perfectly matched, maybe even gave rise to, his most abiding ambition.

Throughout his life, Bill Clinton has had no want of friends. It is only a modest exaggeration that Clinton has met and knows nearly everyone in Arkansas. From kindergarten through collegiate experience on two continents and fourteen years in public life, he has grasped friendships, has held on to them, and has kept them in constant repair. When he ran for president, he had hundreds of exuberant friends in every state, and he clutched for more—friends, and not mere hands—everywhere he went.

This book is about those friendships. It is the idea of Miller Williams, the director of the University of Arkansas Press, himself a friend. Clinton and his brilliant wife, Hillary, seemed too facile, too eloquent, too complete to be real to most Americans, and Williams thought that the personal recollections and judgments of those who were close to them would give them human dimensions. Williams asked me to assemble and edit the volume should Clinton be elected president. That being soon after the Gennifer Flowers and draft eruptions, when the notion of Clinton's election seemed laughable, I agreed. As an old newspaper editorial writer and columnist, I was always one of the mildly professionally disappointed, except at elections, when it was time to judge Clinton against his opponents or against history. Clinton had once telephoned Elaine Dumas to ask why her husband was perpetually so phlegmatic about the governor's accomplishments.

This volume includes one magazine article by perhaps Clinton's most persistent critic, Paul Greenberg, in one of his more sanguine moods, but it is largely the recollections and observations of friends and associates of Bill and Hillary Clinton.

While beseeching people to write these pieces, I began to wonder about the potential value of essays written by people most of whom were close to or who served a politician, essays which surely would be largely a testimony to his goodness. Largely, yes, but the reader will find a rigorous honesty in what some of the closest and most admiring friends have written.

It should be remembered that this is a human, not a political or a historical, chronicle. With Bill and Hillary Clinton more than with most, the distinction between the personal and political is not a bright line. Even so, political traits such as their personal compassion come through in these essays as not contrived, but deeply personal.

The more skeptical reader also may discern, in qualities that are so highly valued by friends, traits that might be disturbing in a national leader. Can a man so sweetly disposed to everyone (except, of late, his opponent in an election) play tough with friends as well as foes? That answer, while it may be hinted at here, will only be found one day in history, and the history of other presidents provides no reliable prologue.

Ernest Dumas
January 30, 1993

Compromise, Consensus, and Consistency

STEPHEN A. SMITH

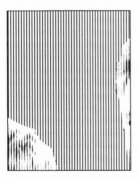 Writing an essay is always dangerous business. The assumptions, ideas, and arguments always reveal as much about the author as they do about the topic, and this fact is not obscured by adoption of a narrative form. When considering an essay about someone with a certain amount of power—oh, say, the president of the United States—the author must be even more aware of certain potential problems.

What are the possible pitfalls, and how might they be avoided? First, both the writer and the reader must be skeptical as to whether the writer's point of view is that of a mere sycophant attempting to curry favor with the prince in hopes of obtaining a place at the court. Second, both must ask whether the account is colored either by close friendship or by strong enmity between the author and the subject, one leading to lax scrutiny and the other to ax grinding. Third, when writing about politicians still in stride, the author sometimes risks either being disappointed in the revealed expectations or disproved by sub-sequent events. Fourth, both author and reader must be aware that writers are not immune to the tendency to recall and recount events in a fashion that overstates the role of, and overplays the importance of, the narrator as actor. Finally, both must ask why the essay should be written and published under any circumstances.

So, aware of the difficulties in telling a tale that is somewhere near the truth, I have decided to contribute my views to this collection of stories about Bill Clinton anyway. Just so you will know and be a bet-ter judge, here's why, and here's what you might want to keep in mind in deciding how much to trust my particular version and vision of real-ity. First, I have only limited interest in joining the civil list and even less expectation of being called to such a position; what I say here is unlikely to enhance my prospects, and I am certain that it will not diminish them. Second, let me confess up front that I am a fan of Bill Clinton. I worked with him and for him in campaigns and in office for almost a decade; I consistently gave him my money and my vote; he was my closest friend for much of that time; and he and Hillary are the godparents of my son. For the last twelve years, however, I have not had, nor do I now claim, any special connection or relationship not shared and enjoyed by every Arkansas citizen. Third, I am now old enough that I am not easily disappointed by people, and I am always at risk of being wrong in everything I write for publication. It is the occupational hazard of all academic writers who have ideas and enjoy intellectual arguments. Fourth, I confess that this will be a personal narrative offered through the lens of my own experience, but I hope that will enrich the story as much as it will undoubtedly distort it. I was in an unusual position to see what many others did not, and I feel sure that most readers will be able to recognize and distinguish the shinola from any lapses in objectivity.

The remaining question is probably the most important. Why should this story be told? Well, there are many ways to tell any story. When the national media tried to construct or reconstruct an image of the real Bill Clinton, there were three Arkansas storytellers ready and willing to provide tales from the dark side in opposition to the enthu-siasm of Clinton's partisans. They were the Arkansans most frequently interviewed by the national media. The cliff-notes version of the plots-in-print by these three newspaper columnists must necessarily lose some of the flavor, but I will try to do justice to the thrust of their thrusts. Paul Greenberg, a south Arkansas journalist who became the editorial-page editor of the only statewide newspaper, the *Arkansas Democrat-Gazette,* soon after Clinton began his campaign for president, whined that Clinton's public career was totally without principle, that there was "no there there," and he claimed to have invented the nickname of "Slick Willie" to represent a lack of moral center in that career. John Robert Starr, the managing editor and chief political columnist of the *Democrat-Gazette,* contended that Clinton was a natural liar, that he would climb a tree to tell a lie when he could stand on the ground to tell the truth, and that he would jump over the moon to tell a lie if it would advance his political career. In his view, there was a center, but it was to satisfy ambition instead of to advance any principles of the public good. John Brummett, a political columnist for the *Democrat-Gazette,* saw it a little differently. He seemed to think that Clinton had begun his career as a brash champion of everything liberal, had jettisoned his values, and had been reduced to a paltry practical pol by having been defeated in 1980. Brummett's opinion was that Clinton would now embrace any scheme or take any stance to stay in office and avoid another term in the political penalty box. These three wise men are equally subject to the cautions I mentioned above, as well as to other motives that can be attributed to passionate political writers for major newspapers, but each usually spins his yarn from too few fibers and too short cotton. They get it wrong, because they don't see it all or get it all. That is why I am sitting at this keyboard, pretending that it is the loom of history, weaving a different tale, and offering a different fabric for the curtain in this rhetorical drama. Again, you can judge the fit.

In March 1971, I was sitting at my desk in the Arkansas House of Representatives when the Speaker of the House, Ray Smith, Jr., of Hot Springs, asked me to come off the floor and meet one of his constituents. He introduced me to a young man named Bill Clinton, who was visiting home during his spring break at Yale University Law School and had already considered the Arkansas State Capitol an important part of that visit home. I was impressed and somewhat envious that he had been a Rhodes scholar and that he now attended Yale law school. He might have been impressed that I was the youngest member of the House, but he later told me he was also slightly annoyed that I had begun a political career in Arkansas while he was still a thousand miles and a few years away from starting one of his own, one which surely put the fabled tortoise to shame as well. Little did either of us suspect at that time how our mutual interest would lead to a close political relationship in that same building.

I did not see Bill Clinton again until June 1972 at the Democratic State Convention. I was a delegate from Madison County and a candidate for delegate to the Democratic National Convention; Clinton was there as a member of George McGovern's national campaign staff to monitor delegate selection. All candidates for delegate from Arkansas were running pledged to Wilbur Mills, but there was more than a casual interest in whom the candidates would support as their "second" choice should the draft-Mills "movement" do as well as expected. In the race for delegate, I was facing two candidates from larger counties, both sympathetic to McGovern, and another who was suspected of latent inclinations toward George Wallace. Clinton suggested that the circumstances favored the latter candidate in the plurality contest and encouraged me to withdraw my name in favor of one of the potential McGovern supporters. I allowed as to how my math was better than his and that he might want to have that conversation with one of the other candidates. Thanks to the work of my political mentor, Charles Whorton, county clerk, I carried most of the delegations from the smaller counties and was elected. Clinton and I then became pals.

We spent considerable time together during the national convention in Miami, and I was thoroughly impressed at how well this twenty-five-year-old Yale student moved among the famous and powerful in the party. I also enjoyed getting to know him and having the chance to talk politics with a kindred soul from Arkansas. We seemed to share a number of views on national issues, such as the futility and injustice of American involvement in Vietnam, and about state politics, hoping that a progressive New South was rising from the shame of the ashes of its racist leadership in the past. I was glad to know that he wanted to come back to Arkansas and to be a political player. I suspected that he would do well, but I had no idea then just how well (or what good) he would do.

That fall I returned to graduate school at the University of Arkansas and made a successful campaign for reelection to the House, and Clinton went on to Texas to continue with the McGovern effort. We talked by telephone a few times during the campaign that became a blowout for Richard Nixon. That spring I encouraged Clinton to pursue his plans to secure a faculty position at the University of Arkansas Law School, and I was delighted to learn that he was successful in that effort. I was even more glad that he passed the Arkansas bar examination just in time to represent me in the biennial Madison County election contest—not the one at the polls but the one in the courts. The Republicans were challenging the election results, which seemed to be well fortified by the lopsided count in the absentee box, in a lawsuit called *Reed v. Baker*. Clinton's first action as an attorney was to file an amicus brief on my behalf in that case. We lost the point, but the Democrats still secured a victory in the election, as well as a debt of gratitude to Clinton for his support of the franchise and the party. It was a debt the Democrats would soon have a chance to repay.

In the fall of 1973 I went off to Chicago to pretend to be a doctoral student, while Clinton impersonated a law professor and pondered his political future. Those were exciting times for everyone interested in politics, as Spiro Agnew copped a plea and resigned in shame, as the *Washington Post* deciphered the Watergate labyrinth, as Nixon dribbled out tapes and had Robert Bork sack Archibald Cox. When I came home for Christmas, Clinton was well on his way to reaching a decision to challenge John Paul Hammerschmidt for the congressional seat from the Third District, and I wholeheartedly encouraged him to do it.

On February 5, 1974, Bill Clinton announced his candidacy for Congress. In his opening speech he declared, "The overriding issue of this campaign is clear; we need a stronger Congress." His campaign literature echoed the theme, "We must elect men to Congress who are not afraid to take responsibility for the future of our country." While the first argument was a reflection of the contemporary political crisis, the second might be read as the germ of his recent call for responsibility both in the presidential campaign and in his inaugural address. He led a field of four candidates with 44 percent in the primary, then handily defeated State Senator Gene Rainwater in the runoff two weeks later.

The issues articulated during the primary campaign reveal both similarities and differences between that campaign and Clinton's most recent run for the White House. He led with a pledge to "give the highest priority to improving the quality of education," because it would bring "more rapid economic growth, a higher standard of living, and the general enrichment of people's lives." Next he called for tax reform, claiming that "the average working family carries too much of the tax load" and that the tax laws encouraged and rewarded corporate investment in low-wage countries. He also addressed the need for public-works funding and warned against the dangers of concentrations of power in uncaring government bureaucracies and irresponsible private corporations. Those issues and arguments are still prominent in Clinton's vision for America, but other issues stressed then—inflation and the energy crisis resulting from the oil embargo—were tied to the particular times.

I was excited by his campaign and the primary victory. When I returned to Arkansas for the special legislative session that summer, I arranged to have Clinton invited to address the House. It was a rousing good time for the Democratic majority, and I still cherish a picture taken that day of Clinton, State Representative Paul Van Dalsem, and me talking and framed by the photographer beneath the motto over the door, "In God We Trust," as if that were a last hope. I was full of hope for the future and sat out the fall term in school to work as a campaign volunteer in charge of issues research, speech writing, media coordination, travel aid, and generally whatever needed to be done at the moment. I believed.

Events, especially the resignation and pardon of Richard Nixon, also shaped the issues of the general election campaign in 1974. The first speech to which I contributed was Clinton's keynote address to the Democratic State Convention in September. He framed the issues of the fall campaign, opening with a blast at Gerald Ford's pardon of

Richard Nixon, then attacking the Republican administration's record on economic issues during "six long years" and their impact on "small businessmen, family farmers, working men and women, the poor, and the elderly." He closed that theme by suggesting, "In the face of this sorry record, if President Ford wants to pardon anybody, he ought to pardon the Administration's economic advisors." He grounded his proposals for needed changes by placing the solutions in the voices of citizens he had met during the campaign. "In short," he said, "in the words of a friend of mine who works on the Scott County road crew, 'The people want a hand up, not a hand out.'" The only problem, he said, in words resonant with his most recent bid for national office, was that "the good Government we love has too often been made use of for private and selfish purposes. Those who have abused it have forgotten the people."

Hammerschmidt's political popularity in the district was based upon his successes at the pork barrel and his skillful use of publicity through newsletters and questionnaires. Clinton confronted the questionnaires issue in the convention speech and throughout the campaign by suggesting that the people never responded with requests for votes against their interest, citing, for example, votes to uphold vetoes of water and sewer construction funds or education funding. In a series of weekly news conferences, he also contrasted his positions with Hammerschmidt's voting record in such areas as agricultural policy, education, public-works projects, and programs for senior citizens.

Hammerschmidt responded that Clinton was a liberal McGovernite, was a tool of big labor and special interests, and was distorting his voting record. Clinton's position on Vietnam also became an issue in the campaign, with opposition supporters manufacturing the rumor that Clinton had perched in a tree at the University of Arkansas to protest the war in 1969. It was the type of campaign that Clinton would face again, but in the future he would fare better than he did in the congressional race in which he carried fifteen of the twenty-one counties but lost by 6,000 votes out of 170,000 cast.

It had been a wonderful, if unsuccessful, campaign. Two days after the loss I received a note from Clinton in which he wrote, "You and I started this together, ended the poorest losers, waiting for a newer day. I am filled with gratitude and affection and no regrets." My feelings exactly. In that campaign, an experience of more than four months of eighteen-hour days, I had learned much about politics, much about the people of Arkansas, and much about Bill Clinton. I had first been impressed by his knowledge of such a broad range of issues and by the energy he devoted to the task, but I soon came to regard him as one of the most intelligent and thoughtful people I had ever met in public life (and I still think he is). Energy and reflective judgment in combination to that degree are rare qualities, indeed. I would spend a week—probably over one hundred hours—reading and analyzing documents and data related to a particular campaign issue; in briefing him on my conclusions, I found that he absorbed it all in the first pass, remembered every statistic, and drew conclusions that I had missed. I also found myself able to anticipate his responses to what was important and why it mattered, making the job of speech writing a breeze, even if the set texts seemed weak by comparison with the speeches he was able to deliver without notes at any civic club or coffee shop in the realm. I came to trust his political instincts and respect his principles, never questioning his motives or integrity on matters relating to the *res publica.*

It was also during that campaign that I first met Hillary Rodham and developed a deep respect for her political commitment. I saw her display of awesome intelligence and observed a fascinating political partnership at work. During the next eighteen months my friendship with Bill and Hillary deepened outside the context of campaign politics. I respected them for their professional competence, was impressed by the extent of their reading, and came to enjoy their quick wit and ready humor. They were my friends, and it was a pleasure to know them.

In 1976, I was hoping that Clinton would make another campaign for Congress. He had maintained and extended his political contacts in the district, had come so close in 1974, and would, I hoped, be running on a ticket with Jimmy Carter. He seriously considered that, I think, but the open seat for attorney general was more appealing. Why, I asked, because it would be an easier campaign? Was it an office that could make a real difference in people's lives or merely one that was a convenient public forum for the time being? No, he said, convincing me that it was important. I again became a campaign volunteer, this time with the title of campaign manager, although in fact Clinton was always his own campaign manager.

The 1976 campaign was the shortest in Clinton's career; announced in March and over in May, he won a clear majority in the primary against two opponents and faced no Republican opposition in the general election. The victory was clearly a result of Clinton's superiority as a campaigner, combining the articulation of issues, unbounded personal energy, an adequate media campaign, and a strong traditional organization advantage.

The obvious plan was to build on the organizational strength in the Third District. Clinton won clear majorities in fifty-one counties, led the field in eighteen other counties, and finished second in the remaining six. One of his opponents, Secretary of State George Jernigan, Jr., later quipped that he would never again run against someone with three hometowns. Personal-contact campaigning and public speaking by the candidate were supported by respectable direct mail, campaign literature, outdoor advertising, considerable radio time, adequate newspaper ads, and minimal television coverage, primarily a thirty-minute interview on campaign issues.

Clinton's persona was one of energy and dedication, captured by the slogan, "Character, Competence, and Concern." Even for such a low-visibility office, he articulated a platform that included minimum prison sentences, victim compensation programs, improved work release, and rapid assistance to law enforcement agencies in interpreting the new criminal code, issues related to criminal justice and the office. More politically revealing, however, were his points calling for fair utility rates, citizens' rights to consumer protection in small claims courts, effective antitrust laws, and a right to privacy. These were issues that revealed a political stance intended to "significantly improve the quality of life in Arkansas" and which were directed toward a constituency group that in 1992 would be labeled "the forgotten middle class."

Clinton called the attorney general "the guardian of our people's interests" with "a broad range of responsibilities." He said, "I want to shoulder these responsibilities." His campaign literature stressed his educational qualifications, even revealing that he had been a Rhodes scholar, and balanced his past work for housing assistance and affirmative action with membership in the Jaycees and the Baptist church. In explaining his commitment, he said, "For years I have worked hard to acquire the knowledge and habits of discipline necessary to do this or any other job well. Every person I will hire to work in the attorney general's office for you will have to demonstrate the same devotion to excellence and willingness to put in long hours. Every decision will be the product of these forces and not of political pressures." As far as I know, that is all true. He did not present himself as anything other than what he was.

The campaign renewed my faith in Clinton's devotion to duty as he saw it and in his abilities as a tireless campaigner. The only policy speech to which I contributed was a Law Day address on "Free Press and Fair Trial," in which he championed the First Amendment and proposed several solutions for harmonizing and maximizing the strengths of the often-conflicting First and Sixth amendments. It was a political talent that I would come to see more fully in the future.

It was also during this campaign that I discovered my first philosophical disagreement with Clinton. He announced his support for capital punishment during the taping of a television interview. While that issue was more important to me then than it is now, his position was one in which he has believed for quite some time and is not one later developed for political expediency in the presidential campaign or in response to Michael Dukakis's political vulnerability on the issue in 1988. On another political issue that year, totally unrelated to the duties of the attorney general, I had hoped he would publicly endorse the campaign to change the state's so-called right-to-work law, but, for reasons we never discussed, he did not take a position on the issue. That decision cost him the endorsement of the state AFL-CIO, but it was because he would not support their position, not because he had misrepresented his own. At a political level, I also found myself disagreeing with Hillary on two occasions, once on a matter of overall campaign strategy and once on a particular tactical choice. I developed a strong admiration for her persuasive abilities and, thereafter, found someone else with whom to disagree.

When Clinton took office as attorney general, I bellied up to the public trough and went to work on his staff, and there I had the opportunity to watch him work. He applied the same energy to public service that he did to political campaigns, and the results were impressive. Consumer protection activities and recoveries increased; the office issued a record number of official opinions; new divisions were funded to control energy rates and to investigate antitrust violations; Clinton chaired a new board to protect individual privacy vis à vis information in government records and produced several publications explaining the Freedom of Information Act for public officials; he supported victim compensation legislation, called for regulation of lobbyists, and issued opinions against state regulations restricting price and professional advertising. He headed a national panel on the rights of the elderly and testified against age discrimination. It was a record of which he could be proud—and one on which he could and would be elected governor. In September, only nine months after Clinton took office, that wise and skeptical columnist, Bob Lancaster, was already opining that the governor's office was his for the taking, a United States Senate seat was a real possibility, and the national ticket was not out of the question for 1988 or 1992.

During the two years I worked for Clinton in the attorney general's office, I did not disagree with any of his public positions or official acts. There were times that I wished he would do more, be bolder (perhaps, on reflection, reckless is a more appropriate word), make or take on additional battles. But those were choices for the attorney general to make, and he was still the most active and progressive public official in state office at that time. He probably always has been since he was elected in 1976. It is certain that we could have had worse—and have had.

Clinton announced his candidacy for governor in March 1978, with a speech filled with optimism as well as tradition. "As a people, we have come a long way in a little time. We have put aside so many of the fears and prejudices which crippled us in the past. But we have held fast to our heritage of proud individualism, love for nature's bounty, and firm faith in hard work, discipline, and respect for each other . . . Our best days are before us if we will forge our own destiny." He stressed a theme in that speech that I believe has been consistent in all of his campaigns, including the latest one. "Most important of all," he said, "I will try to bring out the best in all of us. From this day forward, I will campaign with that goal in mind. I will try to be honest about what cannot be done, but I will direct our visions toward what must be done."

The campaign was virtually flawless, although some would contend that the opposition was not particularly formidable. Clinton swept to a clear victory over four opponents in the primary and embarrassed the Republican scrub in the general election. Despite the ease with which he won, he campaigned as vigorously as he always had. His campaign literature offered a fairly detailed vision for stimulating economic development, helping senior citizens, improving health care, moderating utility rates, promoting family farms, preventing chemical spills, building and improving roads, strengthening public education, and revising the state's constitution. Perhaps these were safe issues, but they were neither easy ones nor inconsistent with his past (nor present) political goals.

In a personally revealing campaign message, Clinton expressed a feeling and a commitment that I believe to be very honest on his part. "All my life," he said, "I've wanted to be involved with people and help them with their problems. I've been very interested in all kinds of people. Politics has just given me a way to pursue my interest and my concern on a large scale. I've given it all the energy and spirit I can muster; I've tried to bring out the best in people through politics; and I've really been very happy doing it." I believe that was true then, and I think it is true today.

Clinton delivered a wonderful inaugural address, again calling on the best in the people of Arkansas, then he plunged into trying to fulfill the promises of the campaign. That effort did not lack energy, but it sometimes lacked the appropriate political craft. He secured passage of an overwhelming portion of an ambitious legislative package; he appointed a record number of women and minorities to his staff and to public boards and commissions; he assumed leadership in several national organizations; he assembled a committed staff with considerable policy skills but often with less sensitivity to the political consequences of the policies they were advocating (I certainly include myself in the group less sensitive to political realities); and he generally did much more than he received credit for doing and later received more blame for consequences that he could not have anticipated or which were beyond his control. Nonetheless, Clinton's first term as governor was quite productive and successful in many ways, and that is sometimes forgotten because it failed to be endorsed by the voters when he stood for reelection in 1980.

Frank White ran a simplistic and often negative campaign against Clinton that fall—Cubans and car tags—and the campaign staff underestimated its impact until it was too late to respond adequately. As a consequence, Clinton learned several valuable political lessons, not the least of which was that negative advertising, regardless of how irrational it might appear, must be countered, and that lesson has served him well in all subsequent campaigns. Other lasting insights that have shaped his subsequent leadership style were the need to involve a wide range of interests and players in the policy process to assure its practical formulation and successful implementation and the need to build consensus and support before enacting policies and revenue measures (exemplified by the near-perfect public campaign for educational reform and financing and the later public campaign for ethics reform).

Clinton's detractors have argued that the election loss in 1980 made him too cautious or even led him to abandon his basic political principles, but I think the first of those conclusions is mistaken and the second simply wrong. The first group seems to define leadership only as approaching problems without consulting the people and enacting clever programs that have no public demand or support, seeing anything less as a weakness. Well, friends, that approach didn't work in the first term, and no one with a lick of sense thinks it will work now. The second group seems to have concluded that a change in leadership style or a new set of goals after 1980 reflected a loss of principles. Wrong again, I think. Trying to enact programs clearly rejected by the voters would be at least unwise, if not foolish and arrogant, and it would be more indicative of a lack of imagination than a consistency to principles. Time and Ronald Reagan·changed many of the rules (seldom for the better for the people of Arkansas and the rest of America), and those changes required new goals and strategies to implement even constant principles. Only an idget or a columnist with no experience on the hustings or in the government would conclude otherwise.

I also argue that leadership can take many forms, and that a change in style does not necessarily mean a change in political principles. This is a truth that I offer for free, although it was a difficult lesson for me to learn. One thing that I realized too late in my time as a member of Clinton's staff was that his approach to conflict and controversy was much more sophisticated than my own. I saw political choices as representing the dialectic between opposites, while he was more sensitive to the nuances or differences and shades of opinion. Where I assumed that zero-sum choices were the only option, he saw the possibility for greater consensus and sought the advantages for compromise among competing interests.

In many ways Bill Clinton's ability to comprehend competing interests and empathize with different parties is, I think, one of his greatest strengths as a public servant; however, this same quality is often seen as one of his greatest weaknesses as a political leader. More than once, I saw groups and individuals who had got a full and fair hearing subsequently feel betrayed by lack of support for favorable action on their requests because they had assumed that the absence of "no" meant "yes." That happened partly because supplicants for support are always inclined to hear what they want to hear and partly because they were not explicitly or immediately told what they did not want to hear. This interplay of motives and assumptions causes problems almost as often as it solves them, although the problems are more often the results of mistaken perceptions than of intentional deceptions. Believing in the power of rhetorical realities, I would anticipate both great promise and significant problems from such a style of presidential leadership. Public leaders and journalists are equally capable of misunderstanding signals that do not conform to traditional patterns of certainty and resolution.

To those who claim that Bill Clinton is Slick Willie, without any principles, I respond that they are quite mistaken, for a close analysis of his rhetoric and his record lays those principles bare, even if they are not the same principles held by these critics. To those who claim that he had changed or forgotten his principles, I argue that his political principles are the same in 1993 as they were when he articulated them in his first campaign for public office, that a change in means does not necessarily reflect a change in ends. To those who claim that he is consistently dishonest, I urge them to listen more closely and more carefully.

The roots of Clinton's approach to national politics were evident in the speech he gave at the Democratic National Convention in 1980, and it is much like the argument he advanced in his own campaign for president in 1992. "We must speak," he told his party, "to the millions who are not here—who do not even watch us on television or listen to us. Who do not care. Who will not bother to vote, or if they do, will probably not vote for us. For it is these people who will decide the election of 1980. And they cannot be moved by the symbols and accomplishments of the past." The party has proven its commitment to equality and justice, he told the delegates, "But now we must prove that we offer more in the way of creative and realistic solutions . . . and that we have a vision that can withstand the erosion of special-interest politics that is sweeping the land."

He warned that the party could not win simply by "putting together the old elements of the Democratic coalition and repudiating Ronald Reagan." He suggested answers that would "ring true with millions and millions of Democrats and thoughtful Republicans." They would be found in the words and works of "a new generation of Democratic leaders . . ." Admitting that the country faced serious problems that other politicians might ignore, he cautioned that the country didn't get into the difficulties overnight and would not emerge from them instantly. He drew on the 1936 presidential election. Franklin Roosevelt succeeded, he said, because "people knew what sort of vision he had for America." He continued, "They knew what action he was taking to transform the country. And they were willing, most importantly, to accept hardship for the present because they believed they were part of a process that would lead them to a better tomorrow."

Clinton then asked the key questions. "What is our vision—what is our hope? We must speak to the American people who do not listen tonight. First, we must say forthrightly that we are in a time of transition, a difficult and painful time from which no one can escape the burden, and in which no one can avoid a responsibility to play a part. Secondly, we must say we are committed to the economic revitalization of America, but it will require a revitalization of our basic industrial structure."

Bill Clinton's principles have been consistent. He has always believed in the need for people to take responsibility, the need for economic opportunity for all to share in the American dream and the need for fair laws and equal justice. He has an abhorrence of racism and all forms of discrimination. He thinks everyone should have the chance to realize dreams and to be able to believe in hope. He loves politics not for personal financial advantage but as a means to advance the collective public interest. He has always articulated his vision for the future. His approach to seeking solutions is now different from the approach that he embraced in his early days in politics. He has learned to listen, and he has come to understand that compromise on details can advance principles more than can uncompromising failure. It might be only half a loaf, but, while it is not cake, it is not an empty plate, either.

I have known him as a friend, and I have appreciated him as a public servant. His greatest strengths are his intellectual capacity, his concern for average citizens, and his love of people and politics. He has not always approached problems as I would have, and his way of doing things has not always been successful. He certainly does not pick fights unnecessarily, nor does he run from those that are unavoidable. He has been frustrated, and he has frustrated others. He has disappointed others, and he has been disappointed with himself. He has sometimes misunderstood people and events, and he has been misunderstood. He has made mistakes, and he will make mistakes. But he always wants to do right and to do good.

That said, I think Bill Clinton will be a damn good president, and he has given me new hope for the future of the republic. That's enough.

Hope: Intimations
of a President

BOB LANCASTER

In creating his political autobiography during the Democratic National Convention in July 1992, Bill Clinton made much of his roots in "a place called Hope." Again in November, in his election-night victory speech, the hoarse and exhausted president-elect remembered where he'd come from; he had drawn his strength for the grueling campaign, he said, from those roots in that place called Hope.

Strong roots they may be, but they run awfully shallow, as indeed do all of the roots in the southwest corner of Arkansas where Hope abides.

The Arkansas component of the area where three states conjoin, called the Arklatex—a flat expanse of ancient sea bottom now dotted with small towns separated by pine forests and cow pastures and drained sluggishly by the sluggish Red River—wasn't settled until the second decade of the nineteenth century, only a little more than a century before the future forty-second president was born there. Only three or four lifetimes ago, it was new country—a quiet arboreal wilderness, broken only rarely by small, grassy prairies, and very, very sparsely inhabited by Caddo Indians. The Caddoes, kinsmen of the storied Pawnee, who rode the plains farther west, were an agricultural people, wonderful artisans, who lived peaceably in scattered riverside hamlets around the Arklatex. But only a handful of them were left by the time of the arrival of the American settlers. Epidemic diseases had decimated them—diseases no doubt introduced by the first European explorers among them in the previous century— killing four of every five of them, leaving a remnant population of perhaps no more than fifteen hundred. They offered little resistance to the encroaching Americans, who came shoving and whooping and banging on pans.

The modest Caddo claims in the region were extinguished by 1835. By then, Arkansas had become a United States territory, pruned away from Missouri, and most of the arable land lying between the Ouachita and Red rivers had been grabbed up by farmers moving west from the exhausted cotton lands of Georgia and the Carolinas and Alabama. Nearly all the immigration into southwest Arkansas was by southerners "goin' West." They came by boat, up the Mississippi and the Red (some detoured up the Ouachita to avoid the Great Raft, a swampy, often impassable, one-hundred-mile-long clog of trees, mud, and debris that stoppered the Red above Shreveport, Louisiana), or they came overland from Tennessee and Kentucky through Missouri on the Southwest Trail, a stump-pocked rumor of a road that twisted down from St. Louis to Little Rock and on to the jumping-off landing called Fulton on the Big Bend of the Red, where that russet stream, eastbound through Texas for five hundred miles, turns south for five hundred more through Louisiana.

Most people in the great expansionist tides were Texas-bound, even before there was a Texas, or they were "gone for California," but those who stopped and stayed in southwest Arkansas built their own little communities to supplant those of the Caddo. Hope wasn't one of those communities, but Washington, Hope's predecessor as Hempstead County's hub town, was.

Washington grew up, starting around 1820, at a place in the Hempstead County woods where several Indian and pioneer trails crossed, eight miles from present-day Hope. A frontier settlement, it became in the 1830s a place of sojourn for adventurers on their way to Texas glory: Sam Houston plotted, or at least mulled over, the war for Texas independence at Washington; Stephen F. Austin, as a young territorial judge, held the first court in Hempstead County in a log building destined to end its days as a slave family's house; Jim Bowie was around long enough for a Washington blacksmith to craft his famous knife; Davy Crockett dallied on his way to the Alamo. In the 1840s, would-be soldiers gravitated to Washington to make up ragged volunteer units that marched away to the Mexican War. In the 1850s, those who gathered in Washington were wagoneers bound for the California gold fields by the southernmost route. In the 1860s, the little town filled with refugees fleeing the Civil War, and it became the state capital for the rebel side after the federal army captured Little Rock in 1863. But it was the settlers rather than those sojourners who give Washington its character, that made it a place that might one day produce a president.

In its July 20, 1992, issue, *Time* magazine, in a mean-spirited essay by the journalist Garry Wills, peered disdainfully at the place called Hope and ventured a historical characterization. "A bleak history," it solemnly declared, basing the assessment on three incidents:

> a Gilded Age governor, "the state's most famous demagogue," was born only twenty-five miles to the west. [More "famous" than Orval E. Faubus?]
> at another place, also twenty-five miles away, a few freed slaves were murdered after the Civil War.
> and twenty-five miles to the south, diggers in an old cemetery in the early 1900s found a few old bones showing that black people in the region long ago suffered horribly from malnutrition.

All events that, at the time they occurred, were at least a day's travel from Hope, in different counties—events as irrelevant to the development of Hope's character, as unilluminating of it, as events that might have occurred at the same time in China or Paraguay.

Sometimes, when you don't know a place but you have an opinion or an impression of it that you'd like to bolster with a historical joist or two, you go scrounging in unlikely places and make do with unlikely scraps. *Time* would have done better understanding Hope, and would have had an easier and pleasanter time of it, by looking just over Interstate 30, an easy fifteen-minute canter to the little town that was Hope's progenitor or earlier incarnation—especially to the Washington of the 1840s and 1850s, when the town was in its efflorescence.

Those who settled down in Washington then, as opposed to those luminaries who passed through, were mostly small-time farmers, some with a relatively small number of slaves, most with none; and a motley of tradesmen—hoteliers, apothecaries, tavern keepers, dry-goods merchants, printers, tinsmiths, blacksmiths, and livery men—and a handful of "professional" men: preachers, doctors, and lawyers. It was a community dominated by men, white men (though free blacks were among the tradesmen, and seem to have been well thought of), who were described by someone who lived among them as "genial, generous, free-hearted men, full of the milk of human kindness, with a vein of humor in their natures, fond of a practical joke, and ever ready with a story or anecdote to entertain or amuse the crowd."

At least two things about the community suggest that it might someday turn out a Bill Clinton: How many of those lawyers there were; and how crazy all these people were for politics, which was their chief public entertainment, and was for the lawyers much more than that. A town with fewer than two thousand residents in 1860, Washington had *twenty* resident lawyers. At least a dozen of them are lionized in the Arkansas annals, including Grandison D. Royston, "grandiloquent Grandison," Zachary Taylor's cousin and the first grand old man of Arkansas politics; and Augustus Garland, a home-grown, just-getting-started youngster who would one day become attorney general of the United States under Grover Cleveland, the highest an Arkansawyer ever got in executive politics until Bill Clinton.

There was a great enthusiasm for the law and for lawyering among these frontier barristers. For the older ones like Royston, it offered the only hope of distinction; and for the young ones, it offered the only way out or up from the coarse and sometimes stultifying life that provincial villagers were too often heir to. The law let a man develop a professional personality and style, and politics gave him a bigger venue for showing them off.

A lawyer in a town not far from Washington, Arkansas, described the attraction of lawyering in 1853:

> Those were jolly times. Imagine thirty or forty young men collected together in a new country, armed with fresh (law) licenses which they had got gratuitously, and a plentiful stock of brass which they had got in the natural way; and standing ready to supply any distressed citizen who wanted law, with their wares counterfeiting the article . . . The clients were generally as sham as the counselors. For the most part, they were either broke or in a rapid decline. They usually paid us the compliment of retaining us, but they usually "retained" the fee too . . . The most that we made was experience.

Actually, nearly all of them made good livings and were the most likely men in communities like Washington to get rich. They prospered not so much by courtroom practice as by land speculation. The ownership of most of the land in antebellum Arkansas was disputed, often by many claimants, and the lawyers who didn't grab off great acreages for themselves made hefty percentages on lawsuits filed for and against those who did. One element of their keen interest in politics was the desire to manipulate—either judicially or legislatively—the government offices and agencies that finally decided the disposition of Arkansas real estate.

The politics of the antebellum period was fluid and volatile. Most Washingtonians were Jacksonian Democrats in the 1840s, but many were Whigs, and the literate and thoughtful weekly newspaper, the *Washington Telegraph,* founded in 1839, was boisterously Whig. Then Whiggery died in the 1850s, and the Democratic party was shattered by the slavery question. Into this developing political chaos, Albert Pike brought to southwest Arkansas the American party, the Know-Nothings; and there was fierce competition among all the factions. Pike, incidentally, had won admission to the bar in Washington, Arkansas, in 1836, and still horsed down occasionally from his big place in Little Rock, or his booky hideaway in the Ouachita Mountains, to argue cases in the Hempstead County Circuit Court. Monumental, ursine, he cut a colorful figure, along with such parochial political stalwarts as Uncle Billy Moss, who was called "the butt-cut of the Democracy"; and peglegged Squire Bill McLellan, so tough that he was adjudged to have won at least a draw in the encounter with the wild stallion that bit off one of his legs at midthigh.

Spirited politics. A candidate for Hempstead County state representative in 1844 was given to removing his shirt at speakings and asking the crowd to gaze upon his back, this to disprove an opponent's contention that the man had been convicted of larceny in Tennessee and flogged at a public whipping post before coming to Arkansas. In spite of his unscarred back's testimony, he lost.

There was never more interest, never more fervor, in Hempstead County politics than in the campaign of 1860. A barbecue and political speaking at Washington that summer drew a crowd of more than five thousand people, who listened closely to speakers representing three of the four major presidential candidates: Douglas, the northern Democrat; Breckinridge, the southern Democrat; and Bell, of the constitutional Union party, which was made up mostly of quondam Whigs looking for a new home. Only the message of the nascent Republican party wasn't heard.

Many years afterward, a man who'd been a youngster in Washington at the time told how the community reacted when it learned that the Republican party had won:

> Never was news of a political contest awaited with deeper interest. In due course of time—I think it was the third day—intelligence of the result reached Washington. Abraham Lincoln was chosen. The announcement fell on our little community with the awfulness of a death-knell. In all previous election contests, the news of the result had been received with shouts of joy by a portion of the people, and good-natured expressions of disappointment by another portion. But here there were none to rejoice—unless we except the bondsman, and his rejoicing was done in silence and secrecy, if at all.
>
> The entire male population assembled at the post office before the arrival of the stagecoach, and when the intelligence was given

out . . . a feeling of sadness, as if some great and overshadowing
calamity was about to happen, pervaded the entire community.
With leaden hearts and down-spirits the little knots of men finally
dispersed to their homes.

The first railroad (now named the Missouri Pacific) pushed
through Hempstead County in the 1870s. It bypassed Washington and
left the little town stranded, insofar as agricultural and commercial
development were concerned, for the remainder of the nineteenth century. The railroad knitted southwest Arkansas to the rest of the United
States, giving people a new way of getting about, and getting goods
about, with mind-boggling quickness and convenience; and new settlers and new businesses in the region hovered close to this lifeline.
And the people and enterprises of Washington gravitated to it, too—
to the point of nearest access to it, which became the town of Hope.
In the last quarter of the nineteenth century and the first quarter of the
twentieth century, Hope drew old Washington into itself.

As Washington faded, one of its lawyer-politicians made a brilliant
career that could be said to have foreshadowed that of the future president. This was Augustus Garland, whose life Bill Clinton's would in
many ways parallel. Raised in Hempstead County, Garland went back
east to Catholic colleges for his higher education, as Clinton later went
to Georgetown University. As Clinton later would, Garland returned to
Arkansas to teach school for a brief time before entering politics. In the
political chaos of the 1850s, he searched for a while for a political identity before finding one. He dabbled with Whiggery in 1854, made
speeches for the Know-Nothings in 1856, supported the constitutional
Union man for president in 1860. He was one of those saddened by the
news of Lincoln's election, but as a delegate to the 1861 convention in
which Arkansas voted to leave the United States, young Garland's was
a clear, strong voice against secession. Among the fire-eaters, his was a
calm voice for conciliation. He nonetheless became one of the state's
first delegates to the Confederate Congress, and, toward the end of the
war, he was elected to the prestigious Confederate Senate.

After the war, he moved on to Little Rock and thereafter made the
state capital his political base, just as Clinton would. A Democrat

now for the duration, he was elected United States senator from Arkansas in 1867, but the Radical Congress refused to seat him, and so he came home and ran for governor and was elected in 1874, one hundred and four years before Clinton assumed the same office. Still only thirty-five years old, he was, as Clinton would be, the Golden Boy of Arkansas politics. He proved to be a resourceful and courageous governor in a time when the state was financially ruined and nigh hopeless, and when its government was in real danger of literally being blown away in a revival of an intrastate civil war. The time wasn't right for a southerner to be regarded as a rising national political star, but young Governor "Gus" Garland—brainy, handsome, with political gifts transcending sectionalism—probably would have been that southerner if the time *had* been right.

He was the first Arkansas governor to give priority attention to improving the state's "image," and he actually made some progress in that task, despite terrible odds, the realities of Arkansas life being what they were then, which is to say, dismal when not actually frightening. Bill Clinton, of course, inherited this challenge in his time, and maybe with his election to the presidency has finished with it. Maybe the image and the reality of life in Arkansas have finally caught up with each other, or achieved a kind of equipoise, so that this old "issue," a heavy burden on this state since long before it even became a state, will be discovered to have been palliated, dissolved at last, during the Clinton presidency, except perhaps vestigially in holdouts for stereotypy like *Time*.

After two terms as governor, Garland went to the United States Senate in 1887, and was in his second term in 1885 when President Grover Cleveland named him attorney general. He generaled for four years, lacking two days, his tenure marked by several crackling legal controversies now long-since forgotten. Some presidential tussles are remembered after a century, but not those of an attorney general. It was thought that Cleveland would put Garland on the United States Supreme Court, but, though two vacancies occurred during those four years, the president finally chose other men to fill them.

Garland returned to Little Rock to practice law the last ten years of his life, and he died in 1889 soon after a stroke felled him while he was arguing a case before the United States Supreme Court. Garland County, where Bill Clinton's other hometown, Hot Springs, is located, was named for him. If, in its infancy, Hempstead County in southwest Arkansas could turn out so cosmopolitan and accomplished a politician, it seems hardly surprising that with another full century to work with, it might bring up another young fellow from much the same mold who would finish out the political progression and capture the presidency.

Memories from Hope

MARGARET POLK

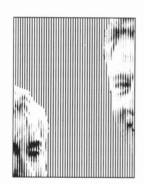 **B**ill lived across the street from us when he was four years old. He'd ride his tricycle up and down the sidewalk, always wearing a cowboy hat and cowboy boots. He often played with our daughter, Mitzi, who is two years older than Bill. One day, Bill let Mitzi wear his hat when they were playing on the slide in his back yard. Mitzi was about to slide down when the string on the cowboy hat got hung up on the side. Before we could get to her, Bill climbed up the slide and pushed her feet up in order to free the string. He was such a little thing then, and I think that showed he was thinking beyond his age. Bill Clinton just seemed to accept responsibility early—even at the age of four.

DALE DRAKE

When Bill was two years old, his mother went to school at Shreveport and at New Orleans, leaving him with his grandparents, Eldrige and Edith Cassidy, who ran a little grocery store. Bill often went to the store with his grandfather and played with the children who lived nearby. His grandfather taught him never to be ugly to anyone, and he grew up with a love for people. There was nothing abnormal about his childhood except that he applied himself at a very early age: Bill could read by the time he was three years old.

BRACK SCHENK

For two years Bill Clinton lived with his mother and stepfather across East Thirteenth Street from my wife and me and our oldest daughter, Betty, at Hope. I vividly recall Bill racing up and down the sidewalk on his tricycle or bicycle, over and over. Bill nearly always had his cowboy boots and cowboy hat on, and he would be on that little bicycle, leaning over like he was riding a racing bike or a wild bronco, churning down the sidewalk as fast as it would go.

Everyone's Friend

GEORGE WRIGHT, JR.

My recollections of Bill Clinton take me back to the time when we were five years old and he and I were in Miss Mary Perkins's kindergarten, a half-block from my house.

Bill was easily the biggest child in our age group. We have a tendency to associate big with clumsy, and maybe Bill was not as coordinated as the rest of us, but while he was bigger than everyone else, he also wanted to be everyone's friend. It upset him if someone in any group that he went into didn't seem to like him. It would trouble him so much that he seemed to be asking himself, "What have I got to do to make this person like me?" I can remember that from when I was six years old. And everyone did like him. He was just a nice kid.

Another thing I remember distinctly from kindergarten was the day Bill broke his leg. All of us had toy six-shooters and cowboy boots, but it seemed like Bill wore his boots all the time. He was wearing them one day when the kids on the playground were jumping rope. Someone talked Bill into jumping. One of the boys—I don't think it was me—tightlined the rope, and Bill tripped and broke his leg. Back then, doctors put a cast on a broken leg all the way up to the hip, so Bill lay up in the hospital a long time with his leg suspended straight up in the air.

A friend of mine has a picture from our kindergarten days with Bill in the middle, and gathered around him on either side are Richard McDowell, Larry Thrash, Joe Purvis, and myself. Bill is pictured with his arms around all of us. He still has that sensitivity. It is what made him, even at five years old, a natural politician. He knows, of course, that in politics not everybody will like him, but I can tell that it still hurts when people say derogatory things about him.

After Bill finished the first grade, his stepfather, Roger, moved the family to Hot Springs and joined his brother in a Buick dealership. Bill and I didn't see each other regularly again, but my family often took vacations on Lake Hamilton at Hot Springs, and Bill would come out to the lake and stay a few days with us at the cabin and we would ski. I didn't see much of him after he went off to Georgetown, Oxford, and Yale, until he came back to Arkansas to teach at the University of Arkansas Law School at Fayetteville and to make his first race for office, in 1974, against Congressman John Paul Hammerschmidt.

When Bill decided to run for attorney general in 1976, Hope attorney Charlie Walker and I took him around Hope and to the little towns around Hempstead County, introducing him to people and doing the kinds of things one does in elections.

One well-known and amazing thing about Bill Clinton is his memory. When I was squiring him around in the attorney general's race, we ran into a friend of mine in the lobby of the Citizens Bank at Hope, and I introduced them. The conversation lasted only a few moments. Two years later, I happened to be in Little Rock with my friend, and we went by the Capitol. Bill came out to see me and recognized my friend immediately. "Hi, Jake," he said. "I met you down at Hope when I was running." Needless to say, my friend was impressed. Of all the people Bill has run into across the country over the years, you'd think he'd get confused, but he never does. Myself, I don't have enough room up there for all that stuff. But Bill Clinton's mind seems to have a boundless capacity for knowledge, especially when it involves people.

From the Playgrounds
of Miss Mary's

Joe Purvis

 I was fortunate to have been born in the cradle of civilization, otherwise known as Hope, Arkansas, between the Red and Little Missouri rivers, and to have been a member of the now-famous Kindergarten Mafia, the class of 1951 at Miss Mary and Miss Nannie Perkins's school, which graduated, among others, Bill Clinton.

There was optimism in 1951 in Hope, a town of nine thousand people just north of the Red River. We had won World War II, and we lived in a town where everyone knew everyone else. It bred a sense of responsibility, because if you misbehaved your mama knew it before you got home.

Everyone seemed to be much the same in Hope. No bridles were placed on anyone's dreams. Mack McLarty, from the same kindergarten class, became president of one of the largest gas companies in the United States and chief of staff to the president of the United

States. Vincent W. Foster, Jr., of the same postwar generation in Hope, is the deputy White House counsel. David Watkins is director of the White House Office of Administration and Management. John W. Walker is one of the South's leading civil rights lawyers.

Hope had two daily newspapers, the *Journal* and the *Star,* and two movie theaters, the Saenger and the Rialto. The Rialto had wooden floors that creaked when you walked down the aisle. The doors were hard to open for a five-year-old boy, especially if you had a soda pop and popcorn in your hands, and if you had not kept your ticket stub, the usher would make you spend another dime on a ticket to get back in. What a gyp! I did not shed a tear when the Rialto closed.

Because there was no television, we spent the evenings at the show, ballgames, or watching Missouri-Pacific passenger trains come through. In the summer, we walked down to Cole's Double Dip for a side-by-side double dip of any of more than twenty flavors of ice cream. An old Coca Cola sandwich board at the intersection of Main and Second streets announced the baseball games between the formidable local semiprofessional team, the Hope Legionnaires, and the teams from nearby towns.

Billy Blythe, as Bill Clinton was known then, lived with his grandparents. My dad traveled for the Equitable Life Insurance Company for up to three weeks at a time, and we lived with my grandmother four blocks from Billy's house. My memories are of evenings spent running on thick St. Augustine grass with no shirt, shoes, or socks, chasing other kids or lightning bugs.

Arkansas had no public kindergartens in 1951, but my folks, Billy's grandparents, and quite a few others valued education enough to enroll the children in the private kindergarten on East Second Street that was run by Miss Mary and Miss Nannie Perkins.

The kindergarten was in a little white frame house, a scaled-down model of the old one-room schoolhouse, with a bell atop the steeple. Kindergarten was in a large room, and there was a coat room in the back.

It was accepted that "the leaders of tomorrow's free world are on Miss Mary's playground today."

Gilbert Stuart's painting of George Washington hung on the wall. The president looked a lot like Miss Mary, who was regal, white-haired, and about the age of the portraited father of our country. Miss Nannie was shorter, nervous, and often a little impatient with Miss Mary. Miss Nannie doubled as secretary of the Hope First Methodist Church, which meant I encountered her six days a week.

We were let out at recess to play and to give Miss Mary and Miss Nannie a chance to relax before returning the hooligans to their parents. One recess provided one of my most vivid memories of Bill Clinton.

Someone had enticed Billy into jumping rope, one of our favorite pastimes. Sometimes the kids who held the end of the rope would pull it tight and trip the person who was jumping. Billy was jumping rope when someone tightened the rope, caught the heel of one of Billy's cowboy boots (The standard attire for boys in 1951 was either blue jeans or blue jean overalls and cowboy boots. In the days of Gene Autry and Roy Rogers, you were not a real boy unless you wore cowboy boots.), and spilled him to the hard, grassless ground. He sobbed uncontrollably. Five-year-olds being sensitive creatures, we yelled for him to get up. He cried even harder and still did not get up, so we began our gentle efforts to comfort him. "Billy's a sissy, Billy's a sissy, Billy's a sissy," we chanted. Miss Mary came out, scolded us, and shooed us away. Bill couldn't stop crying, and his grandmother was called to pick him up. I don't remember, but I'm sure his crying was the topic of whispers and giggles when we were back lying on our pallets.

When I got home that afternoon, my mother asked me what had happened to Billy Blythe at school—because he was in the hospital with his leg broken in four places. Lord, did I feel like a creep! Most of us in the kindergarten had to do penance by marching out to the Julia Chester Hospital and visiting him.

Twenty-six years later, when Bill was attorney general and I was a deputy attorney general, Bill's mother, Virginia, brought to the office in the Justice Building at Little Rock a small black-and-white photograph showing angelic, curly-headed Bill lying in the hospital bed with his leg at a forty-five-degree angle. In the photo, I stood beside the bed wearing a Jughead beanie and a Three Little Pigs T-shirt and looking like a field mouse with a thyroid condition.

People remember little Billy Blythe as friendly and joyous and as a peacemaker. Unlike most little boys, he didn't like to see quarreling and fighting, and he would be the one who tried to break up a scuffle and smooth things over. He wanted everyone to be happy and to have a good time.

Those qualities hadn't vanished when, a quarter of a century later, I got to know him well again. I was an assistant attorney general when Bill was elected attorney general, and I worked in the criminal division the next two years. He infused the whole staff with a sense of high mission, although the work was grueling and the pay was low. We were working seventy hours a week on criminal appeals. Late one evening, as I worked my way through a stack of legal work, feeling overworked and underappreciated, a smiling Bill Clinton slumped down in the chair across from my desk and slid a stick of chewing gum toward me.

"Joe boy, are you having a lot of fun?" he asked.

"What?" I snapped.

"Are you having a good time?" he repeated. "If you aren't having fun, it's time to lay this down and move on to something else. When it becomes hard work instead of fun, it's time to do something else."

People ask me what Bill Clinton was like when he was a kid. When you are a five-year-old, there are only four kinds of people in the world: adults; girls; the bad guys, who are bullies and start fights; and the good guys, who are your buddies and play football, baseball, or cowboys with you or who climb trees and do other neat things. Billy was a good guy.

Bill Clinton is not the product of a blueblood family and an expensive prep school. He is Missus Virginia's boy from the cradle of civilization, who began his formal education at Miss Mary's kindergarten and who's always been a good guy. He became president of the United States when he grew up.

The Music of Friendship

Carolyn Staley

In the summer of 1961, I moved with my parents to Hot Springs and settled into the Baptist parsonage on Wheatley Street. I entered high school as a sophomore in the fall and wanted to meet new friends. Everyone with whom I talked mentioned Bill Clinton, and they uniformly described him as likable, intelligent, talented, handsome, a student leader. One day early in the term, while I stood at a water fountain outside geometry class, Bill Clinton walked up with a friend and said with a smile, "And *she's* going to be my new next-door neighbor." I was surprised and pleased at the news. It was the first time Bill had spoken to me, and I had no idea he knew who I was. I should have known better, because Bill knew everyone in school.

Bill's new house was at 213 Scully Street, around the corner from my driveway, and our back yards joined. It was advertised as an all-electric "Gold Medallion" home, and it showcased all the modern comforts of electrical living. A central vacuum system, with outlets in each room for inserting the hose, allowed you to clean the house without pulling the canister from room to room and plugging it in each time. Amazing! A large master bathroom had a sunken bath, a built-in dressing table, mirrors all around, and a seated vanity area. The house itself was a single-level, ranch-style red-brick structure with white wrought-iron work on the front porch. Two dominating picture windows naturally divided the living and dining areas that constituted the large room across the front of the house. Across the back, through a swinging door off the dining room, was the kitchen, which connected to the den. Off the back of the den was a large patio that the Clintons later enclosed to make a game room. It had a pool table, which Bill and his brother, Roger, enjoyed. Down the hall from the den and living room were three large bedrooms that were for Roger, Jr., Bill, and Virginia and Roger. Rose bushes and other flowering plants covered the yard. Virginia would come home from work in the spring and summer, change into shorts and a tube top, and work for hours in the yard. She always carried a deep tan.

A double carport housed two late-model Buicks: a black, four-door coupe that Bill drove and Virginia's black convertible, which she later traded for a white one. Bill eventually graduated to the white convertible and then took it to Georgetown University for his senior year. But in high school he drove the black coupe, which had high fins on the rear. The Clintons also owned a Henry J, a small, creamy yellow convertible. Bill often took it for jaunts on sunny summer days. The driveway was a makeshift basketball court, where Bill spent many hours alone or with friends shooting baskets at a goal above the carport.

Our neighborhood was quiet and, at first, secluded, although after we left high school more houses were built. From Bill's picture windows and my home you could see a whole city block of peonies, which returned perennially to present us a feast of pink, rose, and deep purple blossoms in April and May.

Along Scully Street were other high-school friends: Mike Karber and the Hassin children, Guido, Anna Ruth, and Florice. Every Christmas Eve, the Hassins, an Armenian family, had an open house for family and friends. Woodrow, the father, was a chef and prepared wonderful ethnic dishes. When Guido died of cancer in 1990, Bill and I went to the funeral and then to the house to spend time with the family, as we had often done when we were growing up. While Guido was sick, Bill telephoned him to raise his spirits. Guido's family said it had meant a lot to him.

Across Wheatley Street from my house was the home of Hill Wheatley, who owned much of the real estate in downtown Hot Springs. Behind his house was a pond where Bill's younger brother, Roger, and his friends often fished. A lovely brook flowed into the pond, and there Bill and the rest of our neighborhood gang spent many afternoons walking and exploring.

The other house on Wheatley Street belonged to the Thomases. Mike Thomas was a high-school classmate and a popular football player. Mike was killed in Vietnam.

Music was the first focus of my relationship with Bill. He knew that I was a talented pianist because he had heard me accompany the large Hot Springs High School chorus and ensemble. One day he asked me if I would be his accompanist for the solo competition at the state band festival. We met several times a week at my house to perfect his solo. We never sat around and chatted. The rehearsals were intense. Bill was always serious about his performances and worked hard to win first place. He performed at his peak at the band festivals and, as often as I can remember, he received first-place ratings. He eagerly waited for the judges' ratings and comments to be posted. I usually played a piano solo, and he also wanted to see how I had fared with the judges.

The bond of music tightened into real friendship. Bill often came to my house simply to pass time, sing, and play the piano. He sat on the bench at the upper end of the keyboard, and we named songs and tried to play them by ear. He liked to sing, and a favorite song was "The Green, Green Grass of Home." Other friends dropped by and joined in. We liked folk songs, Peter, Paul, and Mary, and Judy Collins, and we spent hours listening to Ray Charles, Nancy Wilson, Dionne Warwick, Dave Brubeck, and Stan Getz. Sometimes we tried to play the Brubeck pieces, especially "Take Five," on the piano. Bill played recordings of symphonic band music and wished that the school band could play "Chant and Jubilo" for our graduation processional.

He took delight, too, in the accomplishments of his friends. Occasionally, he would slip into my living room and sit down without my knowledge while I was playing the piano. When I finished the piece I was playing, he would applaud. After the high-school chorus in my junior year performed a choral arrangement of George Gershwin's "Rhapsody in Blue," Bill came to me aglow about my performance. His praise always cheered me.

The beauty of music thrilled him, and its discipline energized him. He worked hard to perfect his playing. He was chosen first-chair, all-state band for tenor saxophone and attended band camps in the summer. Through the band, he also amassed a large network of friends throughout Arkansas. Bill was offered at least one music scholarship to attend college, but by then he had already chosen government service as a career.

His musical interest never waned. In impromptu settings—political events, official functions, and gatherings of friends—he fetches his saxophone or picks up an instrument in the band and plays. I was often asked to play the piano at official functions at the governor's mansion. Bill would come by to talk or to sing with people who were gathered around the piano. Almost always at the end of the evening, when the guests had departed, Bill would sit on the piano bench, and we would play and sing, everything from folk songs to hymns. After dinner at the mansion the day he announced that he was running for president, he asked me to play and sing "Amazing Grace," and he sang along. It was a perfect ending to an amazing day.

Bill invited me to sing at all five of his gubernatorial inaugurations in Little Rock, and he usually suggested the songs. At the dedication service at the Immanuel Baptist Church before his inauguration in 1990, he requested that several gospel songs be sung by a black ensemble: "Goin' up Yonder," which was sung at Hubert Humphrey's funeral and which Bill tells me I'm to sing at his funeral; "Then My Living Will Not Be in Vain," which was sung at Dr. Martin Luther King's funeral; and "Holy Ground," which was sung by a white Pentecostal singer who is a dear friend. At his request, I sang "Alleluia" by Mozart at the beginning of the program, and an organist played Bach's "Jesu, Joy of Man's Desiring," a favorite of Bill's, as the Clintons walked up the aisle to the pulpit. Bill handed me a note saying that it was the best inaugural music yet.

High-school friendships sometimes become eternal ones. Certain friends, David Leopoulos, Joe Newman, and others, always remained close. Since Bill's return to Arkansas, we have all had lunch together every month. In the days of our youth, David, Joe, and others would play football with Bill in the back yard. Some mornings Bill would call and ask me to come over with the crossword puzzle from the morning paper, and we would see who could finish first. Bill was always reading something. David's joke was, "Hey, you want to go over to Bill's and watch him read?"

We did things as a group. Except for special events, such as proms, rarely did anyone have a date. We bowled, played miniature golf, and watched a lot of old movies on television—Bill is still an expert on film classics and stars. When we all went away to college, we were excited about getting together during Christmas breaks. Once, David and I went to Bill's house and put up a big "Welcome Home" sign and hid in the closet to surprise him when he came home from Georgetown University. After we moved apart, we shared happy times like weddings and the birth of our children and mourned together the deaths of parents and friends. When my father died in 1987 at Greenwood, Mississippi, where he had his last pastorate, Bill flew in, and the Mississippi State Police escorted him to the church. He walked in with the family, gave an eloquent eulogy, and came home with us. When David Leopoulos's mother died, Bill tracked David down by telephone to a remote village in Italy where he was stationed with the army.

The seeds of a life of public service were planted early in Bill's life. Our principal was Johnnie Mae Mackey, a strong and patriotic woman whose husband was killed in World War II. She worked in the American Legion Auxiliary, held a Flag Day celebration each year, and taught us to revere the flag and to stand when it passed. Her voice boomed her admonitions to patriotism. Service through elected office was considered a high calling, and many aspired to it. John F. Kennedy was president of the United States, the war in Vietnam had not escalated, there had been no Watergate, and cynicism was an unfamiliar impulse. And the decades of cynicism, greed, and lost hope that followed did not drive out the idealism and faith that had been planted in Bill Clinton.

Bill's mother also helped instill those values. An anesthesiologist, she rose early each day and typically was assisting in surgery before daybreak.

Sometimes we were sitting in the living room when she returned at midmorning, tossed down her purse, and began brewing a pot of strong coffee. "I just can't believe . . ." she would say, and relate some injustice she had seen. We would gather in the kitchen and discuss the issue and possible solutions. She treated Bill as an adult from the day I met them. She respected him, discussed issues with him, and entrusted him with more freedom than most of us had. I think she recognized his unique gifts and wanted to give him the fullest range of opportunities.

Bill was chosen for American Legion Boys State and I was chosen for Girls State in the summer before our senior years. We were selected to be the state's delegates to the national convocations in Washington, D.C., where Bill met President Kennedy. Virginia said she could see in Bill's eyes upon his return home that he would devote his life to elected public service. He asked our high-school guidance counselor where he should go to college to learn about foreign affairs, and she suggested Georgetown. He applied and was admitted.

When we got together after our first year in college, Bill said that he had discovered the outstanding educations his classmates had had; he thought surely that all children in the United States were born equal, but that their opportunities, mainly in education, divided them. Some day, he said, he would like to see all the children of Arkansas given his opportunities.

In April 1968 Bill invited me to Washington to visit him during the spring vacation of our senior years. Dr. Martin Luther King had been murdered in Memphis the day before I arrived, but I had no idea of its impact on Washington until I saw from my plane the palls of smoke covering the city and caught glimpses of the fires from the riots downtown. Bill met me at the airport and told me we were going to do some volunteer work in the inner city. We drove to a relief agency, where a red cross was put on the doors of Bill's white Buick, and the trunk was filled with supplies. Each of us got a hat to cover our faces. Few cars were downtown, and we were able to go through traffic signals without stopping. We delivered supplies to the basement of a church where people left homeless by the fires were staying. Bill suggested that we drive around the areas that had been burned and looted. We parked and walked a block or two through smoldering foundations and broken glass. It was as if Bill wanted to get as close a look as he could at this terrible fragment of our nation's history. Neither of us said anything as we walked around. We were numb. I had taken up black-and-white photography, and I broke the silence by remarking that I wished I had my camera to record the scene. Bill was impatient with me because he thought I had trivialized the moment. He asked why I needed a camera. Would I ever forget what I was seeing?

We turned the corner and saw four or five young black men walking down the middle of the street in our direction. We calmly turned around, walked back to our car, and left. Back at his house, he was melancholy. He had learned long passages of King's "I Have a Dream" speech, and he uttered them under his breath. Another of our heroes had been slain—first, John Kennedy, and now Martin Luther King. Bill knew that the fight for equal justice in America still had a long way to go. He knew he could stay on the campus and watch or go into the streets and lend a hand. He knew he had to be a part of the solution.

One of my oldest memories is of the Bible in the Clinton home with a name inscribed on the front: William Jefferson Blythe. Bill is a Christian whose faith has been a vital part of his everyday life. He attended Park Place Baptist Church at Hot Springs as a boy and professed his faith at an early age. His faith has deepened in his adult life. He sang regularly in the choir at Immanuel Baptist Church while he was governor. Although he couldn't attend rehearsals, he was such a good sight reader that he could arrive on Sunday mornings and sing with a single rehearsal. Not long ago he told me that one of the most important books he had read in years was *Mere Christianity* by C. S. Lewis, which chronicled the struggle between faith and intellect that Lewis had experienced. But Bill's has not been an intolerant religious faith. At the services that preceded his gubernatorial inaugurations, he always saw to it that the services and the participants reflected not only the diversity of races and genders in the community but also the diversity of spiritual faiths in the community.

Though we never talked about it, I always knew that Bill Clinton would be president one day, and a great one. He has charisma, intelligence, and drive, and a loving heart and a sense of justice. No matter where he travels nor whom he meets, Bill Clinton remains the person I knew in my youth.

A Preference
for the Future

TOM CAMPBELL

My first impression of Bill Clinton was his name. I had gotten to the dormitory and learned the name of the person who would share my room, Loyola 225. With a name like William Jefferson Clinton, and a hometown of Hot Springs, Arkansas, I thought, he is black. That would really tweak my father, but the possibility excited me—a New Yorker who had graduated from a disciplined Jesuit high school. I didn't want to be with someone just like myself. Soon, Bill Clinton came in with his mother, Virginia, and he was not black but still different and exciting: a southerner, a Baptist, and with a personality that filled the room. "Hey, I'm Bill Clinton," he said. "How're you?" So began a lifelong friendship.

We were both nice guys, eager to get along and to make this work, and so excited about being at Georgetown that it was easy to be friends. The physical circumstances made it even easier. Our room, formerly a ward in the old university hospital, was very large, with a ten-foot ceiling, closets, individual desks and beds, and a sink between the closets. Bill had a fold-up stereo phonograph and a few records. Neither of us had many clothes, a bicycle, a refrigerator, or anything else that would get in the way. We had modest, if different, tastes, and we were eager to be friends and get on with the future.

After a day spent bidding farewell to hovering parents and wandering around the campus together, we attended a dormitory meeting in John Dagnon's room to meet the others on our floor and to learn the rules of the house. The rooms were assigned alphabetically, so our friends from that year had names like Ashby, Billingsley, and Caplan. These were the old days of coats and ties in class, no women in dormitory rooms, and strict curfews. As a class, perhaps as a generation, we were attuned to rules. There were no wild men, alcohol was not a problem, and drugs were unheard of. The legal drinking age was eighteen, and we could always get a beer, though never in the dormitory, and we rarely drank to excess. Bill was a junk-food man; he liked salted peanuts dumped into an RC Cola and Moon Pies, but also peanut-butter-and-banana sandwiches.

We spent a lot of time in each other's company, waiting in lines, meeting people, trading life stories, and talking. Bill wanted to meet everyone. I was willing to limit my circle to the rest of the floor, my classes, and those whose paths I crossed naturally. But he wanted to meet *everyone* and to remember their names. He remembers them all, even now. That prodigious memory and energy were evident in those first days.

The main impression I had of Bill that year was of his wholesome and complete enthusiasm for the place and the natural way he fit in. The Georgetown of those days was much more a Middle Atlantic school than it would become. The regional and religious underpinnings of my youth, family income, and outlook put me naturally at home at Georgetown. Several high-school classmates were there. Bill had none of that, yet he fit in perfectly. Outwardly, he bore no signs of homesickness or loneliness. He was exactly where he wanted to be. He was no country boy lost in the big city. I later decided that this was owing to a fortunate combination of Bill's own natural drive, his mother's insistence on education, and some wonderful mentoring from the people in Hot Springs. The view from there, I would find from visits to Arkansas over the years, was more worldly than I would have thought. Everyone from Arkansas whom I have ever met has a wonderful sense of state identity that is alien to a New Yorker. They are eager to keep those roots and relationships alive even while living in the wider world. Who of us can remember all our classmates in the fifth grade? Bill Clinton can.

So instantly at home was he that Bill ran for president of the freshman class on the East Campus (made up of the schools of Foreign Service and Business Administration and the Institute of Languages and Linguistics) and won. He probably had made the decision to run before he left Hot Springs. His campaign literature from that year and the next foreshadowed what the nation would see nearly thirty years later. He talked about solving parking problems, getting off-campus students involved in the class, and getting everyone involved in decision making. Not a word about confrontations with the university administration and no mention of Vietnam. It was the fall of 1964, and President Lyndon Johnson was running for the presidency in his own right. Congress had adopted the Gulf of Tonkin Resolution a month earlier, but Vietnam was still very, very far away. Bill showed his love of retail politics, talking to everyone, listening to everyone, urging, nudging people a little closer to his position. When we drafted a flier, he didn't sign the master and duplicate the rest. He spent hours over dinner signing every individual sheet that was to be distributed.

Both of us were international affairs majors in the School of Foreign Service and had several courses in common. One was a survey course in Western civilization taught by the flamboyant and theatrical Carroll Quigley, a course that I struggled through and that Bill ate up. Quigley had a profound influence on Bill. A trait that some great men share—Quigley and Napoleon, among others—is the ability to use time efficiently by sleeping little at night and relying on several twenty-minute naps during the day. Bill learned this from Quigley and used it thereafter, as people who tried to keep up with him on the campaign trail many years later would learn. I would come back from class and watch Bill set his big, noisy Big Ben alarm clock for twenty minutes, lie down on his back, and fall asleep in seconds. When the alarm sounded, he would be ready to go.

Quigley's other legacy was his final lecture of the year, when he explained the key to the success of Western civilization. It was future preference. Nothing was more critical to understanding our world, he taught, than the willingness of the European culture to make sacrifices today to secure a better future for the next generation, to prefer the future over the present. Those words still ring from Bill's speeches. Quigley was a fascinating lecturer and taught history with an emphasis on the larger issues and with little reference to dates. The technical limitations in getting water out of gold mines were an important factor in Western civilization, Professor Quigley said, because they forced the Romans to go further afield to capture hard currency. He discussed the methods of harnessing horses as a factor in history and the influence of the stirrup on the fall of the Roman Empire. A problem on his final examination was: "Discuss the history of the Balkan Peninsula from the retreat of the Wurm glacier to the assassination of Franz Ferdinand in 1914."

We were air force ROTC cadets our first semester. It was voluntary and carried no credit, but we enjoyed it. Bill could not march. I had gone to a Jesuit military high school and knew all about shining shoes, Irish pennants, gig lines, and marching. It was one of the few things I could do better than he, and it was fun to teach him to do an about-face. The air force cut the program from four to two years, and Bill and I turned in our uniforms. The army unit was full.

Bill came to my house in New York that Christmas, the first of several exchange visits to our homes. We had a good time. There is a badly lit home movie of my younger sister playing the piano, Bill sitting on the piano bench and blowing the saxophone, and young cousins scampering around.

Life was wonderful that first year at Georgetown. We discovered the city and the other colleges in Washington, especially the many women's junior colleges. We went to basketball games and polo matches. A large population of foreign students gave the campus a wide diversity. My first political protest was a march in front of the Russian embassy to protest the Russian presence in Cuba. The Cuban exiles urged us into that one. The real activists were the upperclassmen who had been down south as freedom riders and teachers. The civil rights movement was still much bigger than the Vietnam War, which would soon displace it.

That summer, I went to Arkansas, my first trip out of the Northeast, and in the airplane above Little Rock I was struck by the fact that I could behold the entire city from ten thousand feet in the air; it was an isolated ring of lights in the darkness. Everything was memorable: the long, sultry ride to Hot Springs in the big Buick convertible, meeting Bill's stepfather and younger brother and his friends Carolyn Yeldell (now Staley) and David Leopoulos, Bill's constant efforts to make me feel at home, skiing at his uncle's place on Lake Hamilton, the long excursions around Arkansas, the endless two-dollar gasoline purchases, the introduction of more friends, and the dawning awareness that Bill Clinton had been *everywhere* in this state.

We had got along so well that it seemed natural to room together again as sophomores. He ran again for president of the class on the East Campus and won. We lived in a cluster of rooms in Harbin Hall. By now, we had steady girlfriends, roommates from the School of Languages and Linguistics. Bill and Denise Hyland, a statuesque blonde from New Jersey, had started dating as freshmen and would be a steady pair through the beginning of their senior years.

In the fall of 1965, the protests that were dominating college life in much of the country barely touched Georgetown. The Jesuits take very seriously their mission to educate leaders, and they made it clear to us that after Georgetown we had an obligation to use our education to some good purpose and to live productive lives. We were there to learn to take our place in the wider world. Going into business was judged a good thing, serving in government was deemed useful; all of the institutions whose reputations were stained during that era were still seen at Georgetown University as honorable places in which to spend one's life.

After having spent the summer of 1966 traveling in Europe and going to school in Dijon, I returned to Georgetown to room a third year with Bill, this time in the more prestigious Copley dormitory. I played club football, and it had become obvious that better organization and fund-raising were needed for the program. The result was "Hoyas Unlimited," a group that brought alumni money into the sports program. Bill got involved in the effort, and though he didn't play organized sports at Georgetown, he became head of the organization and was instrumental in the lasting success of the program, which still exists.

The Georgetown Student Council was elected in the spring of 1967, our junior year, and Bill ran again. Showing the deft ability to find good people to help him, Bill got Dave Matter to manage his campaign. It was a sophisticated operation that tried to reach the entire East Campus student body, including those who lived off-campus. The university would not give us a telephone list, so a group of us took sections of the student roster, called the information operators, and asked for addresses and telephone numbers in batches of five. We made "Clinton Country" roundels to hang from dormitory room doors, pocket inserts for men, and small pin-on badges for the women. All the cutting and coloring was done by hand.

Bill's opponent was Terry Modglin, a bookish nonpolitician who stuck Bill with an early version of "Slick Willie," the nickname given him by political enemies in Arkansas and, later, nationally. Modglin used the Chrysler Corporation advertising campaign, "the Good Guys in the White Hats," and he tagged Bill as the politico and himself as the agent of change. We lost, but not by much. Bill was down for a while, but he showed the resilience he would show after his political defeats in Arkansas. He considered it a lesson learned, and he tried to discern as best he could the reasons he had lost. Losing that election may have been good for him. He could concentrate on his grades, which would help in the competition for a Rhodes scholarship, and on his work for United States Senator J. William Fulbright.

He revered Fulbright, a senator from Arkansas for thirty years and chairman of the Senate Foreign Relations Committee. In many ways, their lives and careers paralleled. Both were bright young men who went east for their educations, to Oxford as Rhodes scholars, then to law school and, finally, back to Arkansas to enter politics. A significant difference was their marriages. Bill Clinton did not marry the hometown girl but someone very much from the world beyond. It was, I think, an act of love as well as of political courage.

When we returned to school for our senior year, Bill and I moved into a house near the campus at 4513 Potomac Avenue, a dead-end street that faced the old trolley tracks. We were with three men who remain some of our closest friends: Jim Moore, an army brat with roots in Kentucky and an encyclopedic knowledge of the battles of Napoleon; Tom Caplan, a friend from our first year at Georgetown with a love for all things Kennedy (he had been an intern in the Kennedy White House) and a gift for phrase making; and Kit Ashby, son of a Texas doctor and a person very like Bill in his regional outlook and love of a good argument. We all had cars that year and mostly led separate lives, me with the yearbook, Bill on Capitol Hill with Fulbright and the Senate Foreign Relations Committee, Kit in the office of Senator Henry M. "Scoop" Jackson of Washington, Jim with full-time work on campus, and Tom with writing.

A huge antiwar rally and march on the Pentagon occurred in October, but none of us took part because we were aiming to be mainstream players and didn't identify with the marchers. Bill and Kit had their positions on the Hill to protect, and they didn't want to embarrass the men for whom they worked. Since the five of us were together only at dinnertime, the dinners became the focus of our divergent views. Bill was concerned about the Vietnam War and what it was doing to the country. His objection was not that the United States was immoral but that we were making a big mistake. He wondered how a great nation could admit that and change course. He thought America was wasting lives that it could not spare. An older friend of Bill's came to visit him while he was on leave from the army. The soldier, a draftee, was a graduate of the Massachusetts Institute of Technology and was cleaning pistols in an armory in Maryland. Was this productive use of a young life? Later, after he was chosen for a Rhodes scholarship, the argument became very personal for Bill. Where was the greater good? What right did a nation have to compel service in a war that did not support a vital national interest? What obligation did he or any of us have to give up our lives for two years or more and possibly forever? These were the questions we hotly debated over dinner on Potomac Avenue.

Those people on the streets and around the Pentagon were no friends of mine. I was going to the marines. I was going to learn to fly, and if placing myself in a little danger was part of the price, well, so be it. Bill was thinking on a much higher level. To him, it was a problem of governing. Apart from his personal situation, he was trying to figure out how a government went about changing its mind.

But life went on for us in a routine way. Bill's stepfather, Roger Clinton, was sick with the cancer that would soon kill him, and he was being treated at Duke University hospital in Raleigh, North Carolina. Bill would drive down to see him occasionally on weekends and return to school exhausted late Sunday night, but he would be up early the next morning.

The second semester of our senior year was unforgettable for us all. In January, the Tet offensive tore apart what fragile consensus about the war still existed. It is hard now to distill pure memory from what has been shaped by all that has since been written and said about that time. We had a television in the house, and we could see the savage fighting in areas that were supposed to be safe and pacified. The pressure on President Johnson to change course was enormous. We had returned from a performance by the Harvard Hasty Pudding Club that Caplan had taken us to, and we sat around the television to watch Johnson announce that he would not run for another term.

Dr. Martin Luther King was slain a week later. This had as profound an effect on Bill as anything else that had happened in his life. He could recite most of King's "I Have a Dream" speech. Bill was more in tune with what King meant to black people than the rest of us were. He had grown up with poor black people. The grandfather who had helped rear him relied on good relations with poor black people for his meager livelihood. He knew that good race relations were essential for the country's health. He had been in Arkansas during the school desegregation troubles at Little Rock, and he had relatives and friends who did not support the black struggle for justice.

Bill used his big white Buick convertible to deliver food to an inner-city church. Carolyn Yeldell was up visiting, and I can still see us now on the roof of Loyola Hall watching the fires on Fourteenth

Street and the columns of smoke march northward on the skyline. I can remember seeing "Soul Brother" being soaped onto the windows of the Georgetown Shop, an expensive clothing store near the campus decidedly not owned by blacks. We stayed close to the campus and each other, not certain what was coming next. The drive home for Easter was unsettling. It took me through northeastern Washington, a part of the city to which we had never before paid much attention.

On June 5, only four days before we were to graduate, Senator Robert F. Kennedy was murdered in Los Angeles after winning the California Democratic primary for president. Bill had been for Senator Eugene McCarthy, but he was convinced that Kennedy had a more realistic chance to win. It was a terrible blow to all of us, even those who were not Kennedy supporters. What kind of country were we about to inherit?

Bill Clinton is the most unprejudiced person I have ever met. I have never heard him make a derogatory reference to a person's race, sex, or physical appearance. Any manifestation of bigotry distressed him.

In the late summer of 1968, when I was a second lieutenant in the marine corps waiting for flight training at Pensacola, Florida, I went to Arkansas to visit Bill before he left for Oxford on a Rhodes scholarship. We drove to a political rally in a small town in central Arkansas to hear a fellow named Jim Johnson, who was running against Senator Fulbright in the Democratic primary, and Johnson's wife, Virginia, who was a candidate for governor. Johnson, a former associate justice of the Arkansas Supreme Court who campaigned as "Justice Jim," was an unreconstructed segregationist who himself had been the Democratic nominee for governor two years earlier and had been beaten by Winthrop Rockefeller, the state's first Republican governor since Reconstruction. George C. Wallace, then unredeemed, was running for president, and the Johnsons tethered themselves philosophically to him. Their campaign literature entreated people to vote for "Jim-Virginia-George." Wallace carried Arkansas with a bare plurality that year against Richard Nixon and Hubert Humphrey. Both Johnsons lost, but on this hot summer evening they had a friendly audience. As the sun went down, a crowd mostly of men in overalls and straw hats gathered around what I remember as a platform or a truckbed to hear Jim and

Virginia Johnson inveigh against the civil rights movement and liberals and deplore the country's descent into sin and perdition under the demonic influence of people like Martin Luther King, who had been dead from an assassin's bullet since April of that year.

When the speeches were over, Jim and Virginia stood in a sort of reception line to shake hands with people who came to touch the hems of their garments. Bill and I had watched from the back of the crowd, but now he said, "I have to say something to that son of a gun." Bill worked his way to the front of the line and, grasping Johnson's hand and holding it, told the old firebrand that he made Bill ashamed to be from Arkansas. Johnson listened calmly and told Bill politely that if he did not like what he had to say to write him a letter. "That guy is really smooth," Bill told me as we walked away. "He didn't get angry or anything. He handled it really well." It made an impression on Bill, and I think he learned something from a person he couldn't abide: how to handle criticism and to avoid confrontation.

Bill had the need and the facility to reach out to everyone. The rest of us were content to have our circle of friends and others we just "knew." Bill wanted to meet everyone, and he wanted everyone in the circle. Twenty-five years later, he would greet by name old classmates with whom I had only a nodding acquaintance. When we look at old pictures of a dance or some other gathering, he will tell stories about everyone there, recall whom they were with, whom they married, and how they are doing. His roommates knew that he could not be relied upon to keep an appointment and that dinner could not be held up for him. There was always someone back at the school or back on the Hill that he needed to talk to, someone whose brain needed to be picked, or someone whose position needed to be nudged. That phase of his life was like that of the gym rat who wants to play basketball so badly that he will spend hours shooting layups, hook shots, and dribbling. Bill was practicing his craft, working on the problems he knew he would face in government.

Did he want to be president of the United States? Of course he did. And why not? Coming as he did from a small state, he did not think it was a realistic possibility, but he certainly thought that he could be like Senator Fulbright. He was going back to Arkansas to make his future.

Despite the bewildering events of the last months at Georgetown, I have happy pictures of those days. We were all anxious to get on with our lives, Bill to Oxford, me to flight school, Jim to the army, Kit to graduate school in Texas, Tom to Harvard. We planned to gather at the house after graduation for a final farewell meal, but the rain poured and somehow it didn't happen. Without proper farewells, we were gone from Georgetown. But we have not been gone from each other's lives. As best we could, we have kept the spirit of 4513 Potomac Avenue alive, and we have taken the Jesuits at their word and all of us have gone on to be productive, good people—really just like we were then. As for Bill Clinton, he is the same man who walked into Room 225 twenty-eight years ago and became my friend. When I watched him preside over the economic summit at Little Rock in the interregnum before his inauguration, I was back at the dinner table sparring with him and the others over something, listening as the world came into our kitchen.

Don't You Know Whose Table This Is?

WILLIAM T. COLEMAN III

Each year, one hundred twenty-five of the country's top students begin classes at Yale University Law School. In September 1970, classes began for an eclectic collection of high achievers who shared the characteristic of being at the core of the baby-boom legion. The post–World War Two generation's consciousness was formed by an era of economic expansion and opportunity and by the idealism inspired by the civil rights revolution, the disillusionment caused by the assassinations of the Kennedys and Dr. Martin Luther King, and the protest and division wrought by the war in Vietnam.

From this crucible, I embarked upon my career as a prospective lawyer with enthusiasm tempered by skepticism and anxiety. I was excited by the prospect of learning a new discipline that would provide the foundation for my future professional endeavors, and I was eager to meet students who were selected not only for their high academic achievement but also for their diversity and outstanding personal traits. At the same time, I harbored some anxiety about my own ability to perform in the fellowship of such a concentrated collection of highly competitive scholastic draft choices.

On top of these worries, the identity crisis of our generation made future career decisions problematic. Should a new lawyer use his skills exclusively to serve the poor and dispossessed, or should he pursue the pedigree and money of a high-powered, big-city law firm, or was it possible to combine the two? It was a dilemma most of us struggled with throughout law school and, often, long after graduation.

We are all familiar with the saying that one picture can tell a thousand words. The circumstance of my meeting Bill Clinton, who was one of my classmates, speaks a thousand words about him.

I was one of ten African Americans in a class of one hundred twenty-five students. From the first day of law school, the African-American students gravitated toward each other and almost immediately began to form close bonds. By the second week of class, there was a "black table" in the cafeteria. This self-segregation was readily acknowledged and accepted by the majority student body, with one notable exception. A tall, robust, friendly fellow with a southern accent and a cherubic face unceremoniously violated the unspoken taboo by plopping himself down at the "black table." His presence at the table at first caused discomfort. Many of the black students stared at him with expressions that suggested the question, "Man, don't you know whose table this is?" The tall fellow with the southern accent was oblivious to the stares and engaged us in easy conversation. He was immensely curious about people. He had an ability, though in an unintrusive manner, to get people to talk about themselves. He was fun and funny, on occasion even raucous. He had the gift of a true storyteller. He could take the simplest event and, in retelling it, turn it into a saga complete with a plot and a moral. He was serious, too, and would discuss social and moral issues with concern, depth, and insight. By simply being himself, Bill Clinton dissolved the unspoken taboo and became a regular and welcome member of the table.

(The unusually close ties that Bill established with the African-American community at the law school lasted well beyond graduation.

Bill maintained an especially close relationship with several of his African-American classmates. Seven or eight years after law school, the wedding at Martha's Vineyard of Lani Guinier, a close friend of mine and Bill's, provided an opportunity for what amounted to a reunion for fifteen or twenty of the African-American students who attended Yale law school during the early 1970s. The only Caucasian members of our class to participate were Bill and Hillary Clinton and John Widerman.)

Developments a bit later permitted me to get to know Bill even better. Through law classes, I had developed a friendship with Doug Eakeley, who shared with Bill the distinction of being a Rhodes scholar. Two or three weeks into school, Bill, Doug, and Don Pogue became aware of a chance to rent a four-bedroom beach house in Milford, Connecticut, a drive of about twenty minutes from New Haven. The house was the summer home of a New York family, which was looking to get some income from it during the off-season. My participation allowed us to pool extremely limited resources and come up with an alternative to dormitory living or renting a New Haven tenement. Since I already knew and liked Doug and Bill and had heard that Don Pogue was a potential four-star chef, I jumped at the chance to live in elegant poverty.

The year that the four of us spent at the beach house in Milford will always be indelibly etched in my memory. Four very distinct personalities from vastly different backgrounds lived in close contact during an important transition in their lives. Doug, a Yale undergraduate and former member of Skull and Bones, was the product of a white, Anglo-Saxon, Protestant, upper-middle-class family. Don came from a blue-collar midwestern background. Bill was the southerner from Hope, Arkansas. I was the African-American son of a Harvard law school graduate. Despite these diverse roots, we shared a love of ideas and of the written and spoken word. None of us was shy. The result was a non-stop conversation in which each of us was—*is*—trying to get the last word.

Even among a group as talented as the prospective lawyers being trained at Yale, Bill began to stand out. The occupants of the beach house and his law-school colleagues quickly realized that he had special promise. He inspired this confidence even though he rejected the traditional routes to success which nearly all of his classmates followed. Most Yale students sought to realize their ambitions, whether they were obtaining an offer from a prestigious law firm, were working on a committee of the United States Senate, or were being invited to join the staff of the NAACP Legal Defense and Educational Fund, Inc., by burnishing their academic and professional credentials. Yale complicates that strategy by not using a traditional grading system or class ranking. Consequently, students compete fiercely for editorships on the *Yale Law Journal* and other law reviews affiliated with the school and for such organizations as Barristers Union (mock trial) or Moot Court (mock appeals argument). While several students in each class are recruited from small, rural states, they rarely want to return to their states after graduation. They join the competition for jobs at the high-powered firms on the East and West coasts.

Bill, however, made it clear from the beginning that he had no interest in joining a prestigious big-city law firm, a government agency, or some nongovernmental entity dedicated to social change in New York, Los Angeles, or Washington. Instead, he intended to return to Arkansas, where he was going to become involved in politics. Although he never expressly said so, I believe that he made the reasonably rational calculation that given his stellar accomplishments—he was both a Rhodes scholar and a Yale law graduate when he returned to Arkansas—it was unnecessary for him to become an editor of the *Yale Law Journal* in order to pursue most of the job opportunities that interested him in Arkansas. By placing less emphasis on his academic pursuits while in law school, he had time to pursue his first love, politics. Although I believe he could easily have been editor in chief of the *Yale Law Journal* had he opted to do so, Bill decided to begin an apprenticeship in politics while earning a license to practice law.

Bill's apprenticeship in politics was an intense one. While at Yale, he worked on the campaigns of a state senator, a mayoral candidate, and a United States senator. Ultimately, he assisted in Senator George S. McGovern's run for president of the United States. Just before coming to law school, Bill had spent the summer working for a Washington-based citizens' lobbying group known as Operation Pursestrings, which tried to cut off funding for the war in Vietnam through the McGovern-

Hatfield amendment. A friend whom Bill met on this project, Anthony Podesta, persuaded Bill (it was an easy sell) to get involved in the campaign of an antiwar candidate, Joseph P. Duffey, who was running for the United States Senate from Connecticut. Just as the rest of his classmates were purchasing their law books and learning about John Marshall, *res ipsa loquitur,* and collateral estoppel, Bill was organizing for Joe Duffey the Third Congressional District, an ethnic blue-collar region where many of the residents spoke Italian as a first language. Bill used the most advanced techniques in organizing the district: data banks, telephone lists, and door-to-door recruitment by students. Although Bill was able to carry the Third District for Duffey, Duffey lost the election.

Meantime, while law school absorbed every ounce of energy I had, I watched in amazement as September passed and October turned into November with Bill having attended few classes and having paid even less attention to the mountain of case law written in what at that time appeared to be an indecipherable argot that had been developed to obscure the uninitiated reader's understanding of the law. The mere contemplation of what I perceived to be a crisis made me anxious for Bill. He, on the other hand, was serene and confident, even nonchalant. I recall many times when I returned from the library at eleven o'clock at night to discover Bill reading a book. I thought I had caught him catching up on civil procedure or torts, but he would shake his head, make a condescending sigh, and point out that he was reading a murder mystery, Schopenhauer, a Thomas Wolfe novel, or a book on foreign policy. Although Bill may have been somewhat casual about his formal studies, he was a prolific reader and had an intense intellectual curiosity about every conceivable topic and discipline. I would go to bed, get up at six o'clock, and find him on the same couch reading a completely different book. He would suggest that we throw a football a bit before he returned to the campaign trail and I returned to class. Magically, before examinations, he borrowed some good notes, mine among them, disappeared for three weeks, and performed quite well. He was the classic quick study.

The makings of the policy wonk were evident during the Yale years. Robert Reich, whom he would later appoint secretary of labor, was one of Bill's best friends. It is impossible to be a friend of Bob Reich without being a policy wonk. Although Bill loved to talk about the strategic aspects of politics and campaigning, time spent with Bob was spent addressing substantive issues: welfare reform, the negative income tax, educational reform, defense investments. Even at a place like Yale law school, people can't maintain a steady diet of substance. So on evenings that began as group discussions, Bill and Bob would end up at a corner table while closing down the pizza shop.

The non-substantive aspects of Bill's personality could not be suppressed for any period. Because Pogue turned out to be a four-star chef and because we had many friends looking for a quick getaway from New Haven, our beach house became the scene of many spontaneously initiated weekend parties. With Bill as a resident, we never had to worry about finding a life of the party. Whether it was telling a story, playing a prank, lending a sympathetic ear, or just plain good conversation, few people are as magnetic and warm. Bill had the rare ability to engage the conversational partner, either by inspiring the person to talk about something about which he or she truly cared or by providing entertainment.

My year with Bill exposed me to some of his formative experiences, which throw some light on his motivations. Bill's father was killed in an automobile accident shortly before his birth. His grandparents, who ran a small grocery store in a predominantly African-American neighborhood at Hope, reared him for several years while his mother pursued her nursing degree. It was a time of great racial turmoil in Arkansas and in the rest of the South. Governor Orval Faubus was one of the southern governors who elected to stand in the schoolhouse door rather than permit integration. Bill always expressed gratitude that his grandparents, though poor and uneducated, believed that segregation was simply wrong. Bill could not understand why children with whom he played every day should not be able to attend school with him. As a child, he had to deal with these issues, not as an abstract principle but as an emotional reality of being arbitrarily separated from friends. Dealing with these issues at an early age caused him to reject racism with a personal ardor that, frankly, I have found rare in people who are not themselves victims of racism.

Bill continued his apprenticeship in politics by serving as one of two statewide coordinators for the McGovern presidential campaign in Texas. Because he had chosen a strategy that was different from that of other classmates and had pursued it so serenely and surefootedly, his colleagues recognized that he was one of the rare personalities who would define an era. Bill never uttered a word about presidential ambitions. Nonetheless, he made it clear that, in addition to his love for his home and his state, the reason he wanted to return to Arkansas was to enter elective politics. Thus, he defined himself at a young age as a politician. This was a rare characteristic, one that he carried with grace, charm, and ease. While Yale was full of people who were interested in the political process and who wanted to be involved in politics, I knew of no one else who at the age of twenty-four was prepared to define himself as a politician. For most of my classmates, such a statement would have been viewed as pretentious and egotistical. But the political aspect of Bill's personality was such a natural part of him that the statement was merely a description of who he was and what he planned to do. Just as you would describe one classmate as a future member of the law firm of Sullivan and Cromwell, you would describe Bill as a guy who was returning to Arkansas and was likely to run for governor or the United States Senate in several years.

What was it about him that made what could be perceived as overweening ambition seem so reasonable and such a natural quality? First, it was his mind. He had an intellect that could absorb facts and analyze complicated information with computer-like precision. When his natural tendency to be curious about everything was directed toward a specific subject, he could function with astonishing efficiency. Then there was his irrepressible personality. Although many politicians understand people and are good at manipulating them, few of them genuinely enjoy interacting with people. Bill always did. Not only did he derive real enjoyment from all his associations, but he was so secure and at ease that he could avoid having his political goals interfere with the nonpolitical aspects of his life. His roles as a friend and roommate were and have remained distinct from his roles as a politician, which has permitted a degree of trust in both relationships. I visited Bill in Arkansas for his last inauguration as governor in 1991.

I assumed that on the evening of the inaugural dinner I would be placed in a pleasant but remote location so that Bill could use the opportunity to enhance important political relationships in Arkansas. To my surprise, I was seated next to Hillary, and my date next to Bill. But it struck me then as typical that he would use the chance to catch up with an old friend from Detroit rather than to maximize the political advantage of the situation.

Bill's political ambition did not intrude unnaturally on friendships. Rather than imposing himself, which is the tendency of many of his political brethren, Bill grows on you. When a great lawyer tries a case, the jury should hardly be aware of the lawyer and his personality because he is merely the instrument that weaves the evidence together in a way that makes the result he seeks seem inescapable. In the same way, Bill established the wide web of relationships that enabled him to run for president without appearing to do so.

His ambition also seemed so reasonable because he had a laboratory where he could legitimately develop his skills. Had Bill Clinton at the age of twenty-five been a son of California, New York, Pennsylvania, or Illinois, the notion of successfully running for the United States Senate or a governorship would have appeared a bit more far-fetched without far more political seasoning because the political landscape in those states was dominated by names like Dirksen, Scranton, and Javits. Arkansas, however, was a part of Bill Clinton in the way that baseball was a part of Joe DiMaggio. His experiences away from the state had expanded his knowledge and horizons in a way that would allow him to make a greater contribution when he returned. The congenial environment of a small state, it seemed to the rest of us, would permit him to develop the contacts necessary to make a serious run for an important office that only well-connected, well-known, and superbly financed candidates could consider in large states. There also was an intuitive feeling that a small state that had every reason to be proud of such a promising young man would also forgive the mistakes and missteps that would inevitably arise from idealism and youth. Thus, it seemed to us that the articulation of political ambitions directed toward an accessible home base amounted to a nice fit rather than being the ravings of a twenty-five-year-old egomaniac.

A quiet but persistent sense of mission imbued him. Bill knew what he wanted to accomplish through political office. He had observed the human potential that was lost by the needless and irrational divisions of racism and by the failure to make adequate investment in human assets. He was acutely aware, and said so, that his own success resulted from his good fortune in having been exposed to the right people and in having had extraordinary educational opportunities. He marveled that fate had not written him a very different script. He wanted to do what he could, starting in his home state, to begin a healing that would prevent the divisions of the past and the lack of a good education from denying opportunities for others. His recognition that his life would be quite different without his good fortunes gave him the zeal of a convert.

Did putting a political apprenticeship ahead of scholastic pedigrees make maximum use of his years at Yale? The proof is in the pudding. Who can name the editor of the 1973 *Yale Law Journal*?

Of Darkness and of Light

DIANE BLAIR

When the national press "discovered" Bill and Hillary Clinton in 1992, my husband, Jim, and I watched the distorted images that often emerged with amazement, amusement, and occasional anger. We were particularly horrified by the assumption made by a few writers that because Jim is general counsel to Tyson Foods, a major employer in Arkansas, and because we have spent considerable time with the Clintons, our relationship with the Clintons is an insidious one.

For the record: Jim and I became friends with Bill and Hillary before Bill held any office, before Jim was at Tyson's, indeed, before they were the Clintons and we were the Blairs. It was a friendship based on mutual interests (books, ideas, education, Arkansas, politics, children) and personal affinity, and it remains so to this day.

We first met Bill in 1972, when both Jim and I had been chosen as delegates to the Democratic National Convention, and Bill was a coordinator in the campaign of Senator George S. McGovern, who would win the Democratic nomination for president. When his delegate-tracking responsibilities brought him to Fayetteville, Bill dropped by my office in the political science department in Memorial Hall, and we headed for the student union for lunch and a visit. I was instantly taken with this friendly and interesting young man, especially with his combination of practical political knowledge and high-minded idealism, and we easily fell into an intense conversation. Suddenly, halfway through lunch, he stopped me in mid-sentence to say that I was making him terribly lonely for the woman he loved, and he began telling me in glowing detail about Hillary. Since it was already clear to me that Bill would be returning to Arkansas and eventually getting into politics himself, I asked why he didn't marry this wonderful woman and bring her back to Arkansas with him. He would love to, he said, but Hillary was so uncommonly gifted and had so many attractive options of her own that he felt selfish about bringing her to what would be *his* state and *his* political future. Since it was highly unusual to encounter a man in the early 1970s who was that sensitive to a woman's potential, this conversation made a profound and favorable impact on me. It also made me eager to meet Hillary, whom, Bill correctly predicted, I would enjoy as a friend.

That opportunity first arose in 1974 when Hillary came to Fayetteville to help in Bill's congressional race, thereby markedly improving the professionalism and effectiveness of our ragtag volunteer efforts. But my friendship with Hillary truly flourished when she joined the law faculty in 1975. As two of the few female faculty members, we were acutely aware of the suspicion with which many old-timers still regarded women in academe, and Hillary's position as one of northwest Arkansas's few "lady lawyers" (as one local judge persistently and publicly described her) made her even more visible and controversial. Both she and I had been raised and educated outside the South and were more accustomed to big-city anonymity than to small-town familiarity. Furthermore, we were both politically aware and active, anxious to advance the status of women, and eager to encourage more assertiveness and ambition in our students. We were equally dismayed by those who underestimated their abilities because they were from Arkansas and those who lowered their sights because they were female, and we considered it one of our chief professorial duties to rout such inhibitions.

Sometimes we didn't know whether to laugh or cry. When a vacancy arose in the position of university chancellor and it became clear that the short list was all male, the Campus Commission on the Status of Women strongly suggested that the search committee add some qualified women. The search committee chair responded that he would try to do so even if it involved "scraping the bottom of the barrel." A local judge tried to prohibit Hillary from hearing the details of an alleged rape even though Hillary, through the Legal Services Clinic that she had established, was representing the accused! My debate on the Equal Rights Amendment with Phyllis Schlafly before a joint session of the Arkansas legislature (for which Bill and Hillary, sitting up hours one night on my living room floor, helped to "prep" me) was covered by the *Arkansas Democrat* with a lengthy women's page write-up describing Schlafly's shrimp-pink suit and my "stunning" beige dress. It was not easy being a feminist in Arkansas in the 1970s, and Hillary and I were very glad to have each other for advice, comfort, and comic relief. Many of our conversations took place during vigorous lunchtime walks or before, during, and after sweaty tennis matches. (Neither of us was particularly good at tennis, but neither of us ever wanted to lose.)

While some misguided souls insist on stereotyping feminists as man-hating, marriage-despising, children-avoiding females, none of these adjectives could ever be accurately applied to Hillary. She came to Arkansas because she loved and admired Bill, their marriage constituted the most solemn of mutual commitments, and Chelsea's well-being is the central organizing principle of Hillary's (as well as of Bill's) life. Even before Chelsea came along, both Bill and Hillary showed exceptional interest in my own children and Jim's three children, all of whom have vivid memories of lengthy, serious conversations with the Clintons on a variety of topics: school boards, science, literature, world events. Perfectly in keeping with that interest, though still astonishing, is the phone call I received from Hillary late in the afternoon on Election Day 1992 after she and Bill had come home from their marathon fly-around to eight states. "We've got to catch up," she said. "First, tell me about your wonderful sons and daughters." And I gladly did so. In September 1979, in the same living room (Morriss and Ann Henry's) where Bill and Hillary held their 1975 wedding reception, Bill married Jim and me, with Hillary serving as best person and with all of our children serving as attendants. Under the Constitution of 1874, the governor of Arkansas is authorized to perform marriages "for the time being." Jim and I have always teased Bill that the reason we worked so hard to keep him in office, term after term, was that we've never been certain of the legal status of our marriage after he left office. (Bill, by the way, has since performed several other marriages and takes great pride in the fact that all are still thriving.) Hillary looks radiant but somewhat plump in the pictures of my wedding, both reflections of the fact that she was pregnant.

I will never forget the joy in Hillary's voice when she told us that she was expecting, nor the relief we all felt that our recent water-skiing outing on Beaver Lake, done in ignorance of Chelsea's presence, had not interfered with this much-longed-for event. Toward the end of Hillary's pregnancy, in January 1980, the Clintons invited us to attend the Sugar Bowl festivities with them in New Orleans. New Orleans *is* a celebration, and we enjoyed both the array of official parties and some fine eating on our own. When we did the customary brunch at Brennan's, the headwaiter made the perfectly logical assumption that the distinguished-looking gentleman with graying temples (Jim) was the governor of Arkansas and that the first couple had brought along with them a handsome young man and his very expectant wife. Bill loved letting Jim be "governor," accepting the bows from the staff, with no Arkansans in the immediate vicinity to speak the truth and spoil our hilarity.

Other parts of the Sugar Bowl trip were not so happy. The Razorbacks were decimated by Alabama, and, owing to a misunderstanding, when our foursome arrived at the official Arkansas box at the Superdome, there were no empty seats and nobody seemed eager to surrender those they were occupying. New Year's Eve was also something less than glittering. When Hillary expressed misgivings about attending any more smoke-filled establishments, we decided to toast the New Year in our adjoining hotel rooms with some special food and drink (milk for Hillary) from room service. By the time it finally arrived, Bill was sprawled asleep on one bed, Jim on another, and Hillary and I sat on the floor watching a Japanese horror movie and toasting the new year.

As it turned out, 1980 brought both the best (Chelsea) and the worst (Bill's defeat for reelection). Chelsea arrived somewhat ahead of schedule. Bill called us from the hospital. Jim and I immediately headed to Little Rock and were there within hours of Chelsea's birth. Hillary was exhausted but ecstatic, and Bill, who was holding his infant daughter when we arrived, was absolutely overcome with adoration and gratitude. In the years since, although the four of us have continued to debate and discuss an endless variety of changing topics, we have usually begun our conversations with "children" talk, they seeking our parenting advice and experience, we reliving the joys of younger children through Chelsea. I vividly recall one summer afternoon in 1980 when the Clintons arrived at our lake house for a weekend visit. They had driven up from Little Rock in Hillary's car, Chelsea firmly strapped into a car bed in the back seat, more thoroughly protected against any possible automobile injury than any other infant I'd ever seen. She was thrilled to be freed from her restraints, and we put her in the middle of a king-sized bed to kick and crawl, while the four of us sat on the floor, guarding the four corners, exulting in her health and infant happiness. We made another unexpected and urgent trip to be with our friends late in 1980 when, defying pollsters' predictions and Arkansas's long-standing tradition of giving governors two terms, Bill was defeated in his bid for reelection. The assorted elements of this upset have been catalogued and analyzed at length elsewhere. All that needs mentioning here is the personal anguish this brought to Bill, who saw all his dreams crumbling just as they were materializing, and the difficulty for Hillary in trying to deal with his devastation. On post-election morning, Bill made some eloquent and gracious remarks, then he and Hillary stood stoically as though at a funeral, accepting the condolences of their many supporters and friends who had rushed to the governor's mansion to be at their side. After this semi-public event, we went out for lunch, Bill half-laughing, half-crying over the country song on the cafe jukebox, "I Feel So Bad I Don't Know Whether to Kill Myself or Go Bowling." Jim and I did what we could to get them to look back at what had been accomplished and to look forward to all the possibilities yet ahead, but their sorrow and shock and self-reproach were almost impenetrable.

Over the next few months, we, individually and collectively, performed numerous post-mortems on the 1980 campaign. Jim and I repeatedly encouraged Bill to take a break from politics in order to enhance his credibility and expand his expertise in another kind of endeavor. I think we always knew, however, that we were whistling in the wind. Bill is interested, genuinely and profoundly interested, in many different subjects, ranging from music to psychology. I recall one night when he and Jim's sister Trish, an emergency-room surgeon, stayed up half the night discussing medical issues from triage to black lung disease. Bill is the most voracious learner I have ever known, and he eagerly extracts information from everyone about their occupations and observations—and he remembers it. But his passion, his calling, is public service, and in retrospect I don't think he ever seriously considered anything other than to try to recapture the governorship and to resume his life's work.

Public service is a commitment that Hillary shares with Bill, and, as with Bill, her sense of obligation to others began in childhood. Unlike Bill, however, she was also genuinely intrigued by the practice of law, and she and Jim spent hours discussing negotiating strategies, trial techniques, new legal doctrines, and the strengths and weaknesses of the state's legal practitioners and jurists.

On occasions that brought Bill to Fayetteville during the interregnum between his gubernatorial terms, I persuaded him to make some guest appearances in several of my classes. He was easy to persuade when he had the time; he loves young people and seemed happy to be back in a university classroom. My State and Local Government students were fortunate enough to hear a recent ex-governor analyze with great clarity and originality the way in which the contemporary Arkansas governorship must meet the expectations both of those who still primarily want a friendly, folksy, accessible governor and of those who expect the professional, sophisticated delivery of more and better services. My Arkansas Politics students heard Clinton's 1980 downfall criticized and analyzed with amazing objectivity by Clinton himself.

Most interesting to me was his impromptu appearance in my Politics and Literature class. This is a course in which students read and discuss novels, plays, and short stories to enhance their understanding of some subjects—ambition, ethics, commitment, and compromise—that contemporary political science tends to ignore. Bill began by briefly discussing several works of political fiction that he thought were filled with important insights: Ignazio Silone's *Bread and Wine,* Robert Penn Warren's *All the King's Men,* Robert Musil's *The Man Without Qualities.* Then he discussed at even greater length what he had learned from his extensive reading of political biography, specifically citing works on Lincoln and Truman, Churchill and Hitler, and Lyndon Johnson. One student asked if politicians should be guided by public opinion. "Great politicians don't give a rip about public opinion," Clinton mused, "but then the same could be said of Hitler or Stalin." The political giants, he suggested, were usually a combination of darkness (insecurity, battles with depression, family disorder) and of light (a sense of history, a desire to serve the public). In the great leaders, the light overcame the darkness. At the end of the class period, there was time for one last question, and a student asked, "Why, considering all your other choices, do you do politics?" Clinton paused, clearly thinking over some elaborate and eloquent answer, and then he simply shrugged and grinned: "It's the only track I ever wanted to run on."

Once back on track when he was reelected governor in 1982, and again in 1984, 1986, and 1990, Bill kept his self-imposed pledges: to keep his legislative goals fewer and more focused and to listen constantly to the people and explain to them why he was taking the steps he was taking. His knowledge of Arkansas and of its people is encyclopedic, and his love for the state is passionate. Nobody who had worked with Bill and Hillary as they persuaded, bullied, cajoled, and threatened the state's public schools onto a higher plateau could ever doubt the amount of brain power, willpower, strategizing, and sheer nonstop stamina these two will put into a worthy endeavor. Jim and I have seen Bill, exhausted from a full round of "off-duty" events (the Tontitown Grape Festival, the Washington County Ice Cream Social, a retirement home dedication, a political meeting on a highway problem—all on a Saturday), arise early on Sunday morning to court a possible industrial prospect who might bring welcome jobs to the state.

Bill often stayed with us when on official business in northwest Arkansas, and in all those years I can never remember a time when he preceded us to bed. I have occasionally arisen at two or three o'clock in the morning to find him still sitting at the kitchen counter doggedly working his way through to the bottom of his big black briefcase. Sometimes we would learn very shortly before his arrival that he was going to be staying with us, and occasionally he just showed up. He knew where we "hid" the key and where we kept the sheets to the fold-out bed in the den. Even after all the children went off to college and there were empty beds, I think he preferred sleeping in the den, surrounded on all sides by shelves of books. The Clintons never expected special treatment, and they were perfectly capable of making their own way around the kitchen. No matter what the occasion or the hour, all evenings with the Clintons ended around the kitchen counter, either in our home or theirs, with Jim and Bill competing against each other to see who could create the most imaginative concoctions and who could tell the most hilarious stories.

Probably our happiest times with the Clintons have been at our lake house, where nobody wears anything fancier than blue jeans and a T-shirt, the meals are as casual as the clothing, and the world gets temporarily put on hold. I have seen Hillary, usually so energetic and self-disciplined, lie immobile for five hours on a comfortable couch, devouring a novel. And even Bill, who never completely relaxes for long, has floated by the hour in a giant inner tube on Beaver Lake with a big unlit cigar in his mouth. In addition to swimming and boating, we have usually found time for games, especially if the children were along: board games, cards, and an occasional game of charades. One does not play the Clintons lightly in charades: It is not easy, I discovered, to act out Sartre's *Being and Nothingness.* Nor does one lightly take on Bill in his favorite game—hearts. Once, one of our daughters had a visiting beau who had acquired doctorates in both mathematics and philosophy by his mid-twenties, and who prided himself on his hearts-playing ability. He was amazed and impressed when Clinton trounced him.

But whether at the lake or elsewhere, what the four of us have primarily spent our time doing together is talking. All four of us, from very different perspectives, have been longtime close observers of public affairs, from global economic developments to county courthouse doings. All four of us share a passion for improving public education. It has been Bill's most consuming legislative priority; Hillary was his indispensable partner in effecting education reforms in Arkansas; I have taught for more than twenty years; and Jim has served on both the state Board of Higher Education and the University of Arkansas Board of Trustees. All of us love to travel and to extract meaning from our observations. All of us enjoy a rousing debate and will sometimes take contrary positions just for the fun of disputation. And all of us are voracious readers with our rendezvous often turning into extensive book swaps. Clearly, we have shared many common concerns and interests, but I doubt that friendship can be reduced to some simple equation of commonality or ever fully explained to those outside the relationship. It is simply something that fortuitously happens, and then is to be treasured as one of life's most precious gifts.

Donna Taylor Wingfield, Billy Blythe Clinton, and Miss Mary Perkins, Hope, Arkansas, 1951

Miss Mary's Kindergarten, Hope, Arkansas, October 1951. Bill Clinton is to the left of the gap in the back row.

Miss Mary's Kindergarten, ca. 1951, Hope, Arkansas. *Left to right:* Randy Murphy, Richard McDowell, Joe Purvis, Bill Clinton, George Wright, Larry Thrash, and unknown

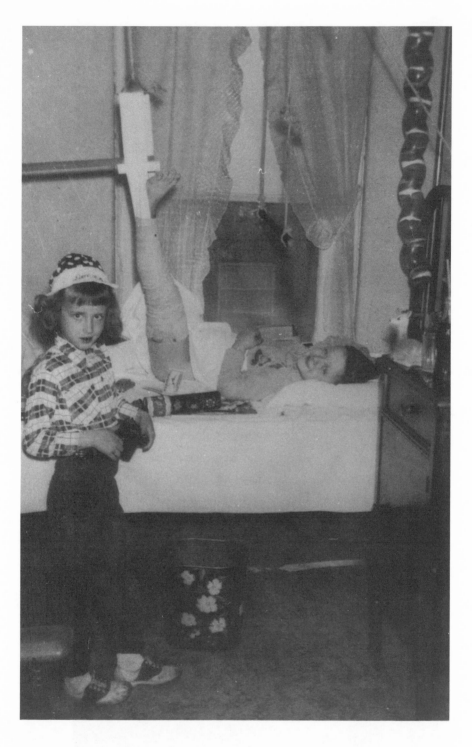

Donna Taylor Wingfield and Billy Blythe Clinton, Julia Chester Hospital, Hope, Arkansas, 1951

Left to right: Kit Ashby, Mary Faith Mitchell Grizzard, unknown, Jim Moore, Bill Clinton, Denise Hyland Dangremond, Tom Campbell, Maurine Miles Murtaga, unknown, and Neil Grimald; beginning of sophomore year at Georgetown University, Fall Festival, October 1965

Bill Clinton greeting new students during orientation, Georgetown University, 1967

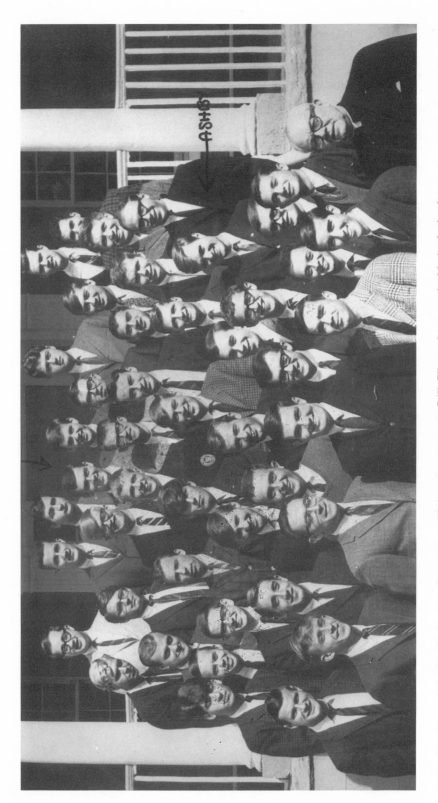

Alpha Phi Omega Service Fraternity, Georgetown University, 1967–68. Bill Clinton is recognizable in the back row.

Left to right: Tom Campbell, Bill Clinton, Jim Moore, and Kit Ashby, at "100 Days" (until graduation) party, March 1, 1968

Left to right: Kit Ashby, Bill Clinton, Jim Moore, and Tom Campbell, Houston, Texas, August 1969

Bill Clinton and Tom Campbell

Bill Clinton and Steve Smith after Clinton's primary victory in the race for Congress, 1974

The young law-school instructor with the poet William Stafford at the home of Miller Williams after Stafford read from his work at the University of Arkansas in 1975

Governor Bill Clinton, Inaugural Day, Little Rock, 1979

Bill Clinton with state Senator Morriss Henry (*left*) and former U.S. Senator Kaneaster Hodges, Jr., in February 1979 at the dedication of many thousands of acres held by the Nature Conservancy to be used for state parks

Bill Clinton, 1980

Bill Clinton "taking the snap" during a staff picnic at the governor's mansion, summer 1980

Bill Clinton, Rudy Moore, Jr., and Sam Bratton

Nancy Pietrafasa and Hillary Rodham Clinton, governor's mansion, 1980

Bill Clinton, Jim Blair, Diane Blair, and Hillary Clinton. Governor Clinton married Jim and Diane Blair on September 1, 1980, with Hillary serving as "Bestperson."

The Clinton tricycle. *Left to right*: former governors Frank White, Sid McMath, and Orval Faubus; Hugh B. Patterson, Jr., publisher of the *Arkansas Gazette*; and Lt. Gov. Jim Guy Tucker (with helmet)

The Clinton Factor

WOODY BASSETT

Anyone in Arkansas planning public events, especially political ones, had to account for the Clinton Factor. At any event he was scheduled to attend, unless it was the first one of the day, Bill Clinton would be late by thirty minutes, often by much, much more. Everyone became accustomed to his tardiness. For more than fifteen years, I have spent countless hours waiting for him to arrive and then waiting for him to finish talking to the last person he could find. He lingered at every event, finding out what was on people's minds and then hearing them out until he was finally pulled away, literally, by an aide who was charged with getting him to the next appointment, long since delayed or else fifteen minutes and two hundred miles away. The pattern became familiar to the nation in 1992 when he ran hours behind as the campaign schedule every day stretched into the midwatches of night. Bill Clinton never wants to leave anyone who wants to talk to him.

His chronic tardiness, it seemed to me, was never thoughtlessness but, on the contrary, a manifestation of his insatiable curiosity, a genuine interest in people, and remarkable physical and mental endurance.

I've never known anyone else with such curiosity. Bill always wanted to learn as much as there was to know about every subject, which earned him the faddish sobriquet of "policy wonk" in the presidential campaign, but his curiosity about people was even greater. He wanted to know people, wanted to know their names and to know about them, and once he knew he never forgot. His memory of people is legendary.

When people are hurting, Bill seems uncannily to sense it, even if he doesn't know them well. In the fury of campaigning and in the moil of crowds encircling him, he could tell when someone had run out of luck. Countless times I saw him reach out to someone and ask how he could help. At a rally we attended a few years ago in Springdale, Arkansas, a teenage girl, sullen and mute, stood alone away from the crowd. Her eyes caught Bill's as he was leaving, already late for his next appearance, and he veered away from the crowd. While the rest of us shuffled impatiently at the door, Bill talked to her for fifteen minutes. As we left the building, Bill handed me a piece of scratch paper with her name and telephone number on it. She was pregnant and unmarried, frightened, and in horrible emotional pain. Bill told me to get her a lawyer and to see to it personally that she got help. It had nothing to do with his powers as governor.

Time is of such small consequence to Bill because his own inexhaustible energy stretches his days. People marvel at his endurance. His secret is that he is the world's best catnapper. He can doze off in the batting of an eye. One day during the furious last days of campaigning for governor in the Democratic primary in 1982, Bill stepped into a side room at an airport. He collapsed into a chair and fell asleep in seconds. A few minutes later, he hauled himself out of the chair—refreshed— and headed for the airplane. He dozed off in my car many times while we sped between events and I conversed with someone else in the back seat. Bill would rouse himself from time to time to inject a lucid and relevant point and then slip instantly again into a pacifying slumber. He might sleep only for ten minutes, but he would awaken at the next stop refreshed and energized, leap from the car while it was still moving, and plunge into the crowd. It always amazed me.

Rather than tiring from contact with people, Bill seemed to gather energy and spirit from them, especially from friends.

Many of us from Arkansas flew to New Hampshire a few days before the presidential primary in March 1992, when Bill's fortunes were sinking and even he seemed dispirited. While the snow fell in Nashua, we squeezed into a junior-high-school gymnasium that was overheated and sticky. The experts had written Bill's political obituary, but they didn't know that he had already come back from the dead more times than Elvis, notably after two political defeats in Arkansas and after the speech that wouldn't end at the 1988 Democratic National Convention. Seated behind Bill and Hillary in the gymnasium, the Arkansas people began "calling the hogs," the cheer that rallies the football and basketball teams of the University of Arkansas. The rest of the crowd was mystified, but Bill knew what it meant. He turned back to us with a face filled with gratitude. Bill arose and told the crowd that these people were friends from home who had come all the way from the heartland to this faraway state to help him in his hour of need. The two small states, he said, had something in common: a proud, independent people. He delivered a vintage Clinton speech. You could feel those people, who had never met him, beginning to connect with him. I knew I was witnessing another resurrection of Bill Clinton.

During my final undergraduate year at the University of Arkansas in 1974, I walked into the lobby of a Fayetteville bank and saw my father talking to a tall young man with hair nearly as long as mine. My father introduced me to Bill Clinton, a law teacher who was running for Congress. But it was Hillary Rodham whom I remember best from that year. On my first day in law school that fall, I took a seat in the criminal law class, and in strode Hillary Rodham, looking, I thought, a little out of place. She neither talked nor dressed like she was from Arkansas. What a culture shock it must have been for her. All of us had heard a little about her. She was Bill Clinton's girlfriend. She had finished her work with the Judiciary Committee of the United States House of Representatives, which had voted to impeach President Nixon. Nixon had resigned the presidency weeks before classes began, so Hillary came to Fayetteville to teach and to help Bill run for Congress. If she seemed a little out of place, it was also abundantly clear that she was tough, intelligent, and articulate. A few were intimidated by her brilliance and others simply resented it. I liked her immediately. People never were indifferent about Hillary. They either liked her or they didn't, but they always respected her. She became an excellent teacher. Her lectures were forceful and organized, and she demanded the best from every student. She would invite discussions of all viewpoints and then follow a careful and logical analysis to a concrete answer.

Bill taught constitutional law the fall semester of my second year in law school. It was clear to all of us that his interest was in politics and government, not teaching, but he was a good teacher in his own way. He lectured the same way he campaigns: conversationally and without notes. Teaching seemed natural and effortless. He was enamored with the history behind constitutional cases and spent most of the class talking or listening rather than asking esoteric legal questions.

We spent three weeks of his constitutional law class discussing *Roe v. Wade,* the landmark decision legalizing abortion that the United States Supreme Court had handed down two years earlier. Professor Clinton was captivated by the case. While he tried to keep his personal political beliefs out of the discussion, it was obvious that he believed in the principles enunciated by the court, particularly the underpinning doctrine that the federal constitution gave everyone a fundamental right to privacy. I often think of that class and how ironic it is that the law professor might have the opportunity to pick the successor to Justice Harry Blackmun, who wrote the majority opinion in *Roe.*

Bill and Hillary were married that fall and settled into their home on California Avenue in Fayetteville. Bill was preparing to run for attorney general the next spring, and I knew, as did my classmates, that he wouldn't be around the law school much longer. Still, most of us would see much of him in the years afterward. We enlisted in his campaigns for attorney general, governor, and president.

But his reelection campaign of 1980 was not one in which I was involved. I sensed that he was in trouble with the voters, but I still was shocked when he was defeated. Watching the returns that night, I was saddened by the thought that his political career was over and that so much talent and promise for the people of my state were lost. Several of my friends went to Little Rock to see Bill the day after the election and reported that he was shattered by the defeat. A couple of weeks later, while I was rushing into Razorback Stadium at Fayetteville to watch the university football team play, someone yelled my name. Bill Clinton was striding toward me. I expected to see a disheartened man. I told him how sorry I was that he had been defeated. "I'm not going to quit," he said cheerily. "I'll be governor again, and I want you to help me get it done." He was already thinking about the future and how he might regain the confidence of the people. I don't remember who the Razorbacks played that day or whether they won or lost, but I won't forget the encounter with Bill Clinton at the stadium.

The call came early in 1982. He had decided to run for governor again and wanted help. Many friends encouraged him to delay his comeback because everyone sensed, as he did, that his career could not withstand another defeat. I harbored that feeling. But Bill and Hillary thought the time was right. He knew that people had to be persuaded that he had learned from his mistakes, and they had to be convinced to give him a second chance. Bill went on television statewide to ask for that second chance.

A political campaign in Arkansas is a full-contact sport, ranking a little ahead of intercollegiate football in degree of mayhem. But Clinton knew that the voters were fair. An election is like a jury trial with no rules of evidence. Bill had taken many hits in the 1980 campaign, and he resolved in 1982 to give as good as he got and to respond to every allegation. "If someone repeatedly spreads lies about you and you don't answer," he told me, "people eventually will believe them."

Bill Clinton plunged into the campaign with a fury and doggedness no one had ever seen. His energy and endurance always gave him an advantage over all his opponents. He worked sixteen to twenty hours a day, seven days a week. No one else I ever knew could keep up that pace for very long without losing his spirit and his faculty for thinking clearly. One unseasonably frosty day shortly before the general election, I picked Bill up at 3:30 in the morning at the home of Jim Blair, a lawyer, and his wife, Diane, a professor of political science at the university. We had attended a number of political events the night before and then settled into a Fayetteville night spot for relaxation and reflection before he finally retired to the Blairs' home for a nap. It was misting and cold when we headed into the night to the Campbell Soup plant, where the shift was about to change. As one shift left and the other arrived, Bill stood in the rain at the plant gate, shaking hands while I handed out pamphlets. Workers obviously were impressed that Clinton had got up in the middle of the night to greet them. After twenty minutes, a woman entering the plant stopped, looked up at Bill, and said, "Mr. Clinton, I was going to vote for you, but now I don't think I can. Anyone stupid enough to be standing here freezing in the rain in the middle of the night when they don't have to, well, they ain't smart enough to be governor." Bill broke up, laughing.

We dashed out of there to meet the shift change at another plant at six o'clock and then sped to a neighboring county for a breakfast and reception at daybreak. Bill had already met more voters than most politicians will meet in a day. I kept going with the knowledge that I would be able to catch up on sleep as soon as he left for other precincts, but he ran at that unrelenting pace for the duration of the campaign.

On the eve of the election, a caravan followed Bill from the Fayetteville airport to a big rally at the campaign headquarters between Fayetteville and Springdale. When we were in the car, Bill asked how I thought he was going to fare in northwest Arkansas. He recalled his exact vote totals from 1980 in each of the counties and wondered if he would do better. For the first time, slumped in the seat of my car, he seemed to be dog-tired. I started to analyze his strengths in the counties when we saw cars lined up and a large crowd on the side of the highway. Suddenly, Bill bounded out of the car and waded into the throng, high-fiving and shaking hands as he went. As we headed back to the airport after the rally, he thought the next day would be a good one. Striding along the tarmac toward his plane at the airport, he noticed another plane taxiing to a stop and realized that the plane carried Governor Frank White, his opponent, whose followers had gathered at the hangar for an election-eve rally. Bill sprinted toward the plane and greeted White warmly as he climbed off. I looked over at White's supporters waiting quietly like sentinels near the hangar and at the people who had followed Bill and were now spilling all over the runway, and I realized that he was right. It would be a good day for him.

The voters swept him back into office by ten percentage points.

Change Has Never
Been Easy

CARL WHILLOCK

A friend on the law faculty of the University of Arkansas, where I was an administrator, asked me early in the autumn of 1973 to go to lunch with several professors and to meet Bill Clinton, a new teacher who had impressed people in the law school. We met as we were climbing into a car to go to a cafeteria in Fayetteville. The conversation in the car and in the cafeteria was about Richard Nixon and Watergate, and it was largely uncharitable. I said nothing until someone turned to me during lunch and asked my opinion. I replied that I had a low opinion of the character of President Nixon, who I believed would turn on his own mother if he saw a political advantage in it. I apparently rose in Clinton's estimation. "There was this conservative guy in a suit and tie over there looking at his plate and quietly eating away, and when he said that, I couldn't believe it," Bill recalled later. "I figured him for a Nixon supporter."

Bill and I saw a lot of each other that fall. My wife, Margaret, and I lived a three-minute walk from the law school, and Bill came by often. Our children formed a lifelong attachment to him. Our daughter Melissa would fix peanut-butter-and-jelly sandwiches, his favorite. He came over to help us move new furniture into the bedrooms and later to help us pack our belongings when we moved from Fayetteville. After moving furniture once, he left his spare shoes in the bedroom, and our daughter Jenny, who was thirteen, came in carrying the shoes. "Bill must have the biggest feet in the world," she said.

Clinton's consuming fascination with politics and with government was evident even in those days. I had been an aide to the late James W. Trimble, who had represented northwest Arkansas in the United States House of Representatives for twenty-two years. Trimble had been defeated in 1966 by John Paul Hammerschmidt, a conservative Republican building-supply dealer who in the next seven years ingratiated himself with Democrats and Republicans alike. Bill had broached the idea of running for Congress in one of our early visits and asked what I thought about it. If he had the urge, I said, he should do it. One evening in late autumn, while we were all sitting on the floor around the fireplace, he said he thought he would do it. I climbed upstairs and got a card file with the names of people from throughout the congressional district who had helped Jim Trimble. Others had asked for my help in earlier years, but Bill was the first person whom I encouraged to run and whom I helped. He says that no one but his mother, until then, had encouraged him. The common wisdom was that Hammerschmidt was invulnerable. He was popular, and the district had been voting for Republicans in presidential elections by widening margins.

If he ran, I told him, he would need to start traveling that quadrant of the state early to meet people who could help him. Congressman Trimble had believed that shaking hands with people, looking them in the eye, and asking them for their support were by far the most effective ways to win votes. I volunteered to travel with Bill a few days to introduce him to influential Democrats in northern Arkansas. I emphasized that he had to start early and work late. We took off at six-thirty on the morning of March 5, 1974. It is a day etched clearly in my memory.

Northwest Arkansas is mountainous; its roads are steep and bending; and the towns are often far between. Bill saw dozens of Democratic leaders that day in towns that stretched out along United States Highways 62 and 65—serpentine little roads that run easterly along the ridges and valleys of north Arkansas—and he never failed to make a good impression. Keep in mind that this was 1974, and bushy-headed and sideburned young men were rare and not much admired out in the woods of the Arkansas Ozarks. Yoked with Ivy League and Oxford pedigrees, Clinton's appearance was apt to provoke not only mistrust, but also dislike. Men like Hugh Hackler were reflexively skeptical of someone of that description who aspired to political office.

Hackler was a semi-retired businessman. He and I, representing two of the poorest hill counties anywhere, had been in the state legislature together in the 1950s. Later, he served on the state's game and fish commission. When Bill and I reached Mountain Home, Bill went handshaking around the courthouse square while I looked for Hackler. I found him playing dominoes under a dim light at the pool hall. When he finished the game, I got him off to the side and said that a young man who was running for Congress as a Democrat was in town and that I wanted them to meet. Hugh said he was committed to supporting state Senator Gene Rainwater of Fort Smith, a conservative trucking executive who had announced that he was running for Congress. I told Hugh that Clinton was a bright young man who would someday be governor or United States senator and that in the years ahead Hugh would want to support him. Hugh agreed to meet him. At the drugstore, the three of us slid into a booth with red and ivory naugahyde cushions and drank coffee and soft drinks. I told Bill that Hackler was committed to supporting Gene Rainwater. Hackler asked Bill where he had grown up. Hot Springs, Bill replied.

"I have a good friend in Hot Springs," Hackler said. "I doubt if you know him. He has some drugstores there. Name is Gabe Crawford."

"Sure, I know Gabe Crawford," Bill said. "He and my dad are good friends. We visit in his home all the time, and he and his family come over to our house."

The conversation went on more warmly. After twenty minutes, Hugh looked at me and said, "Carl, I am going to call my friends in

Fort Smith and tell them I want out of my commitment to support Senator Rainwater and that I'm going to support Bill." Because of conversations like this, I'm convinced that Bill could persuade two of every three voters to support him if he could have one-on-one conversations with them.

We ducked into the Baxter County Courthouse across the street to meet the county officials. One of them was Vada Sheid, the county treasurer. Vada spotted a button dangling from a sleeve of Bill's jacket. While they talked, she cut the button off and sewed it back. The subject of birthdays came up, and they learned that they shared a birthday, August 19. Vada told me in January 1993 that for the next nineteen years after that encounter Bill faithfully sent her a handwritten note on each birthday. Vada was in the state House of Representatives or Senate for most of Bill's years as governor and was always a steadfast supporter.

At Berryville, I introduced him to Reverend Victor Nixon, the pastor of the First Methodist Church, and his wife, Freddie. She became his campaign coordinator for Carroll County. Victor later performed Bill and Hillary's marriage ceremony and gave the invocation before Bill's speech accepting the presidential nomination at the Democratic National Convention in July 1992 in New York.

At Marshall, a town on a plateau above the Buffalo National River, Bill converted Eddie Tudor, whose family published and edited the *Mountain Wave,* the county's weekly newspaper. All of the Tudor clan except Eddie were Republicans. We crossed the Buffalo River wilderness about nine o'clock that night and found the darkened house of Will Goggins in St. Joe, population about one hundred. Will had been chairman of the county Democratic committee for many years and had to be reckoned with in Democratic politics. Will had gone to bed already, but he dressed, came to the door, and invited us in. Bill and Will talked for a few minutes. I believe that Will Goggins supported Bill in every political race he ever made.

We arrived back in Fayetteville a few minutes before midnight. Margaret was excited. She said I had missed some grand entertainment: university students had been streaking on Maple Street in front of our house, and hundreds of young people had gathered to watch this new activity.

About two weeks later, David Pryor asked me to manage his campaign for governor, and I did little else for Bill Clinton that year. Pryor won the governor's race (and later, three terms to the United States Senate), and I became his chief of staff. (Margaret's brother, Rudy Moore, Jr., managed Bill's first campaign for governor in 1978 and became his chief of staff. Margaret, to the best of my knowledge, is the only woman in Arkansas history to have had both a husband and a brother manage the campaigns and executive offices of governors. She is remarkably humble about it.)

After his defeat in the House race that fall, Bill tried to persuade Hillary Rodham to move to Fayetteville. He talked to Margaret and me and other friends about making her feel welcome in Fayetteville. Hillary had worked in his congressional campaign, but she didn't accept a teaching position at the law school until January 1975, and Bill beseeched us again to make her feel good about coming to Fayetteville. He was afraid she would feel out of place. On Hillary's first day in town, Margaret telephoned her and invited her and Ann Henry to lunch at our house. Margaret fixed gumbo from a new recipe, and they talked for a long time.

While Bill was attorney general, the board of trustees of Arkansas State University at Jonesboro conducted a search for a new president, and Bill gave me some valuable help. I was named president at Christmastime in 1977, and for his troubles, Bill was sternly reproached by the state Republican party for using political influence to help a friend.

By the time Bill ended his first term as governor and ran for reelection in 1980, we were living in Little Rock, and Margaret worked in the headquarters of that terribly disappointing campaign. He was defeated—for about a dozen reasons, I believe. He had no control over a few factors: a sour economy in which prime interest rates reached 18 percent; one of the hottest, driest, and deadliest summers on record; President Jimmy Carter's use of Fort Chaffee as a holding place for refugees from Cuba; and the explosion of a Titan II missile in an underground silo near the town of Damascus, which caused widespread fear in central Arkansas. All these things translated into a vague discontent, which focused on the young governor. But a few factors he and his wife could have controlled: an increase in automobile and truck license fees, the alienation of leaders in the huge poultry industry, and Hillary's use of her maiden name after their marriage. A few of his friends spent many hours the next year talking with him about the reasons for that defeat and whether he should abandon elective politics, wait a spell, or immediately run again in 1982. His overpowering impulse was to run that year, and he did. Our notion was that he should address Arkansas people on television, plainly admit the mistakes of his first term, apologize for them, tell people that he wanted another chance, and insist that this time he would do a good job. It was a hard, almost unprecedented thing for a politician to do, but he did it unflinchingly and persuasively.

We had one final serious association. He called me one day in 1987 and asked me to chair a commission that would study ways to make the state's regressive tax system more just. He wanted the commission to hold hearings throughout the state to hear ordinary people say what they thought was wrong with the tax system. We held the hearings and gave him our report that fall. He used it to make some fine recommendations to the legislature and the people. One recommendation was to change the state constitution, which makes tax reform exceedingly hard by requiring 75 percent of the members of each house to approve most taxes. The regressive sales tax is the only major tax that can be raised by a simple majority. We recommended that the constitution be changed to require a level 60 percent to change any tax. Bill made a valiant effort to persuade voters to embrace that reform, but strong business and agricultural interests opposed it, and it was defeated. In 1989, with the high threshold for raising most taxes still standing, Bill tried to increase income taxes on corporations and, in a small way, on high-income individuals. He also tried to eliminate income taxes on the poorest working families in Arkansas, which my commission had recommended. Overwhelming majorities voted for it in both houses—more than enough for the legislation to become law in forty-nine states—but not quite the three-fourths needed in Arkansas. Not until two years later, after defeating a well-financed opponent in a reelection race fought almost entirely over the tax issue, did he persuade an extraordinary majority of the legislature to raise income taxes on the richest corporations for the benefit of youngsters seeking a technical education and to reduce the tax burden of 250,000 workers whose wages were not enough to lift their families above the federal poverty line.

Change has never been easy in Arkansas. I do not think that eager young teacher even imagined how hard it would be when he set out upon a political career that fall in 1973. The amazing thing is that, two decades later, Clinton's exuberance and optimism are still undaunted.

They're Killing Me Out There

RUDY MOORE, JR.

United States Senator J. William Fulbright told me in the spring or summer of 1973 that a young man named Bill Clinton, who had worked for him and whom he admired, would be coming to Fayetteville to teach at the University of Arkansas Law School, and he wanted me to get to know him. I was in the state House of Representatives then, and our proximity in age and our mutual interest in politics and in law made us a natural pair. We became friends instantly. Bill sometimes came up to our house, and we had potluck dinners. He wasn't married then, but everyone soon began to hear about Hillary. One of the engaging things about Bill was his continual mention of a wonderful and cerebral young woman he had known at Yale. None of us had ever met Hillary, but we all had a good feeling about her because he talked so lovingly about her as a person and as an intellectual partner. By the time she came to Fayetteville the next year to teach in the law school, all of us were in awe of her. Due partly to the buildup that preceded them, both quickly came to be very prominent young people in the political, social, and academic culture around the university.

Within a few weeks of his moving to Fayetteville, Bill had adopted a cause. He came to me one day very disturbed because he had learned that physicians in Springdale, where I lived then, were refusing to treat Medicaid patients, and he wanted me to help him change their minds. Poor people who didn't have insurance or who couldn't pay were taken down to Washington Regional Medical Center at Fayetteville, which was the county's public hospital. Generally, poor people simply didn't get medical care until the need became an emergency. Our noble goal and dedicated effort produced little in concrete results and about all that we accomplished was to make a bunch of doctors mad at him—and me.

Not long after his arrival in Fayetteville, Bill began to talk about running for office. Most of us recognized, from the first, his vast political potential. It was evident that he had running for office in mind when he moved to Fayetteville, and that it was only a matter of finding the right office. He never gave any thought to running for a local office or for the legislature; his goals were on a higher level. It didn't take long for him to settle on challenging for the seat of United States Representative John Paul Hammerschmidt, a conservative Republican who, through assiduous service to constituents and a willingness to engage in mutual back-scratching with Democratic leaders, had, in only four terms, firmly entrenched himself.

It was a time of optimism. Many people who had reached adulthood in the 1960s were out to change the world. In Arkansas, there had been a big turnover in the legislature in 1970. Governor Dale Bumpers had an enormously popular reform administration, the state treasury had the first surplus in decades, and the legislature had enacted progressive taxes and a great many changes. Along came this brilliant young man who wanted to run for Congress, and he naturally received encouragement from those of us who wanted more liberal change. It was apparent that if you could get a man like that to be your congressman rather than John Paul Hammerschmidt you would make the swap in a minute. Only a few of us thought that he could actually win such a race, but we were spoiling for a worthwhile fight. To his credit, Bill Clinton relied on his own political instincts and not on the instincts of those who were pessimistic. Even in defeat there was victory, as the November election thrust Bill into the Arkansas political scene where he has been a permanent figure ever since.

For a person in his late twenties, I knew a lot of people because I had served in the legislature, and I introduced Bill around the local communities in the Third Congressional District and made some telephone calls for him. But what he needed was money and visible support from powerful people in the district, and Bill had little of either. At least in the northern part of the congressional district, even Democratic county leaders would not put themselves on the line for him and challenge the incumbent. Because of Hammerschmidt Democratic officials had found that they could, after all, be on mutually beneficial terms with a Republican. A few of the city fathers didn't like Bill because they thought he was too young and too liberal. As the election neared, Bill got some money from the unions, but it wasn't enough. A little money early in the campaign would have made the difference, but he had no political heavy hitters who could raise a few thousand dollars for him here and there. He lost with 48 percent of the vote. Bill had worked literally night and day, and I think he was genuinely shocked that he lost. Most of us were surprised that he had come so close. He had swept most of the rural mountain counties, which was amazing because he had had so little media coverage.

His near-victory against an apparently invulnerable politician was such a phenomenon that it had the effect of a triumph. The political writers toasted him. When Bill Clinton decided in the middle of 1975 to run for attorney general the next year, he was almost handed the key to the office. He carried sixty-nine of the state's seventy-five counties against the secretary of state and the deputy attorney general in the Democratic primary, and the Republicans put up no opponent.

I had only modest volunteer involvement in his races for Congress and attorney general. It was clear that he would run for governor in 1978 because United States Senator John L. McClellan had died and Governor David Pryor was running for McClellan's seat in the Senate, leaving the governorship up for grabs. In November 1977, I wrote the attorney general a letter saying I would like to be involved in his race for governor. He asked me to come to Little Rock for a talk, and he asked me there to manage his campaign. Neither his Democratic opponents nor the Republican nominee were too powerful, and he won easily, but we did achieve something lasting in that campaign. Bill's goal was to forge a strong organization in all seventy-five counties from the disorganized contacts of his first campaigns. We developed a computerized list of people across the state. If we could track down people who gave even one dollar, their names went into the computer. Bill built upon that list in all his succeeding races. It proved its worth in 1992, when he raised more than four million dollars for his presidential race in Arkansas, which has one of the lowest per-capita incomes in the United States.

Bill was an idealist who had a lot of ideas he thought would be good for Arkansas, but I don't believe he ever considered himself the messiah of a poor, benighted state. Arkansas was benefiting from the progressive Bumpers and Pryor administrations; both Bumpers and Pryor had been elevated to the Senate; and Jimmy Carter was in the White House, having carried Arkansas with Bill Clinton as his state campaign chairman in the general election in 1976 by the second largest majority in the country. Those elections and Bill's in 1978 reinforced the notion that there was a receptive political attitude in the state. In the Democratic primaries, Bill talked about improving education and economic development and building rural roads, the staples of Arkansas's political campaigns. The transition to the governor's office began after he won the Democratic party nomination in May because we felt a quiet confidence that his Republican opponent would not be able to mount a serious challenge in November. Work on the administration became intense. Bill put together policy and legislation-drafting groups. He had many, many ideas about energy and the environment. He had a vast amount of information from reading in so many areas. If I had five things on my agenda at any one time, he had fifteen.

He and Hillary had friends from around the country who joined the gubernatorial transition team and later the administration, and Bill recruited people from other states who he thought shared his ideas and could implement them—an earnest young West Virginia doctor, for example, ran the state Health Department and carried out his plan to get primary care to the impoverished rural areas. He also hired an energy expert from Massachusetts and a human services administrator from Tennessee. Bill hired a national accounting firm, Price Waterhouse, to do an audit of some state services, and one of its young executives wound up joining the administration as director of social services. Hiring so many people from outside the state was sure to arouse provincial prejudices, and the administration was roundly criticized. The outside recruitment may have been a political mistake. Some of the personalities did seem to abrade people, even inside the administration. It was one of the elements that contributed to the perception that many people began to have of Bill: that of an arrogant young man who was going to impose his ideas on Arkansas people whether they were ready for them or not. The perception was likely a factor that led to his stunning defeat after only one term as governor.

But the decisive contributor to that attitude was not the "outsiders," Hillary's use of her maiden name after the marriage, or the Cuban refugees who stormed the streets around Fort Chaffee after Bill had acquiesced in President Carter's sending them there, although all of those factors were used effectively against Bill in the campaign. He was beaten by car tags.

Bill had promised an accelerated highway program, and people tend to accept taxes for highways when they will accept them for no other purpose because they can see the tangible fruits of their taxes. Bill had a package of taxes, but the largest part of it, an increase in annual vehicle license fees, couldn't get through the House of Representatives due to the state constitution's requirement that three-fourths of the members of both houses must approve most forms of taxes. Bill's program had placed the largest tax on heavy trucks because highway studies showed that they were not bearing their share of taxes based on the damage they caused to roadways. To get the trucking and poultry lobbies to stop pressuring representatives and thus allow them to pass the program, Bill eventually agreed to a compromise that shifted part of the big-truck share of the tax increase to passenger cars and smaller trucks. Also, the annual license fee for cars was to be based on the weight, not the make or model, of the car.

The political effect was catastrophic, and neither Bill nor the rest of us saw it coming. It was not a matter of dollars—the increases amounted to ten or twelve dollars per car. Those were especially hard times in rural Arkansas. There had been a terrible heat wave and drought that year, and some people had died from the heat. A gasoline shortage created long lines at the gas pumps and also made it difficult for many farmers to obtain fuel. A big strike by truckers frayed nerves. In that environment, starting in July 1979, one-twelfth of the motorists in Arkansas each month stood in line at the county revenue office to renew their licenses, encountered the license fee increases, and returned home roiling mad and complaining to their friends.

It hit Bill in the summer of 1980. He returned from a campaign swing through south Arkansas that had taken him to a Cooper Tire factory and other plants. He came up to me with a terribly pained expression. "Rudy, they're killing me out there," he said. "I go into these factories where people have always been kind to me and they tell me I kicked them in the teeth." I said, "You mean people are mad because they're having to pay twenty-five dollars instead of seventeen?" Bill answered, "No, they said I kicked them when they were down." It was not the amount of the fees, he said, but the fact that the economy was bad, that working families were having a hard time making ends meet, and that he had heedlessly raised their vehicle license fees.

People also told him that the fee structure was unjust. It cost about the same amount to license a ten-year-old Chevrolet as it did to license a new Cadillac because the cars were in the same weight class. Moreover, working people in the rural areas traded old cars every year or even more often, and we had raised the transfer fee for car titles from five dollars to ten dollars. Bill was so chagrined that I knew things were bad. We talked briefly about having a special session to change the law, but there was no clear consensus as to how to stop the political hemorrhaging, so nothing was done.

As I look back, it is more evident that Bill Clinton was not the same person psychologically in 1980 that he had been before or that he has been since. It must have been something personal, perhaps in his relationship with Hillary, but he was ambivalent and preoccupied. Those fantastic political insights had abandoned him. His reelection campaign reflected it. His instincts ordinarily tell him when a campaign is faltering, and he is insistent upon rectifying it. But in 1980, perhaps because he and nearly all the rest of us had presumed an easy reelection, he had people running the campaign who had no experience running a state race. There was bickering, organizational work wasn't being done, decisions weren't being made, and most important, the charges made by his opponent weren't being answered. Bill never demanded of that campaign what he had demanded before and what he has demanded since. He wouldn't make decisions that would bring the campaign out of its lassitude. I remember that Steve Smith came up with a wonderful television commercial that panned from the telephone company building on Capitol Avenue to the state Capitol, a few blocks west. The voice over it said, "The man in *this* building wants to raise the amount you pay when you make a toll call from a dime to a quarter, and the man in *this* building [the Capitol] is going to keep him from doing it." The governor was quarrelling with other utilities on larger but esoteric issues that people couldn't understand, but here was an instance that people could understand where Bill had successfully fought a utility rate increase. Bill wouldn't use the commercial; he thought it was demagogical and unnecessary. This was not a crucial failure, but when it is combined with his refusal to confront the internal problems in his campaign and his inability to think through the car-tag problem, it suggests that he was not the decisive person he ordinarily is.

He was also having trouble with personnel decisions in the government. Two of Bill's and Hillary's friends, a husband-wife team, had left good careers in California to work on Bill's program during the transition and then in his administration. Both were bright and full of ideas, but their personalities and operating styles didn't mesh with the staff's. The situation deteriorated to the point that a group of senior staff members, whom I nicknamed "the gang of five," came to my house one night and said that the situation was intolerable and that I should do something about it since I had the governor's ear. I went to the mansion and told Bill and Hillary, and they recognized the depth of the problem. It was difficult because of the deep personal relationship between the two couples. Bill asked me to terminate them. It was the worst thing I ever had to do. That was a terrible way to handle the termination of jobs that were based on personal friendships, but at that time he simply couldn't do it. It was more evidence that he was not on top of his game then.

Hillary did not seem to be deeply involved in that race either, and she has been crucial in every other. She ordinarily was a perfect balance to Bill, who tended to trust everybody and sometimes to be hopelessly optimistic. She saw the dark side of events, and she could see that certain programs and ideas wouldn't work. She would say, "Bill, don't be such a Pollyanna. Some of these people you think are your friends aren't." But she, like the governor, did not seem to be fully engaged in the campaign of 1980.

Some of his difficulty, both in the campaign and in the office, stemmed from his nature, which was to trust everyone and to want everyone to like him and to see the worth of what he was trying to do. Those impulses and the need to be absolutely certain that he was correct sometimes troubled his decision making, particularly in making appointments. He would gather more and more information on an issue or an appointment in search of a magic consensus. He would be trying to make the right decision, but in the process he would frustrate people who were interested in the outcome. The chief criticism of him was always that he told people what they wanted to hear and then didn't follow through on his commitments. But I never detected any duplicity, and I do not believe he ever acted from cunning or in the pursuit of power or money or even in the pursuit of his own self-interest. He simply wanted to help every person he could, and he hated to disappoint anybody if he thought there was any merit at all in what they wanted. He wouldn't tell them flatly "no." People would leave his office thinking they had a commitment when he had only been understanding and cordial. After a meeting with a group, I would tell him, "Governor, those people think you are going to do what they wanted," and he would reply, "Well, I'd like to do it if this and that would happen." And I would say, "But I think they have the impression you're going to do it even if those things don't happen." He always had boundless confidence in his ability to forge a consensus and work out any problem, if he could just get enough information and talk earnestly to everybody involved. Even with Bill Clinton's extraordinary powers, that's not always possible. Sometimes you must just take a side and make the call. That was against Bill's nature, and that is where Hillary often provided some balance. Over the years, I think, he has shed much of that naivete. After the bitter defeat in 1980, he certainly lost it in campaigning. He said he would never again let campaign charges go unanswered for more than a few hours, and he never did, and that he would match every punch with a harder one, and he always did.

Bill Clinton took that defeat as well as anybody has ever taken defeat. I was at the headquarters that night in the war room. As soon as we got the results from a few precincts in Miller County, in the southwestern corner of the state, Bill knew he would lose. He was winning those boxes but not by the margin he needed. He never complained about the attacks on him, and he didn't blame anyone but himself for the inept campaign. During the weeks afterward, he did a lot of self-examination. How, he wondered, could he have disappointed so many people? He talked briefly again about calling a special session in the remaining days in the interregnum to repeal the hated car-tag fees, but he thought that people would view it as sheer opportunism, and he decided that they would be right. Many postmortems by political pundits and self-styled historians have said he was devastated by his defeat and wandered around for months lost in the wilderness. Not true. I was with Bill and Hillary every day from his November defeat until he left office in January, and I know firsthand that he accepted the vote of the people, he sought to analyze the reasons for the defeat, and he started planning his comeback. He and I and Little Rock attorney Bill Allen gave some thought to setting up a law practice together, but I wanted to get back to Fayetteville and my sons and Bill Clinton knew he wasn't going to practice law but was going to begin the process of planning his political resurrection.

Bill Clinton's intellect, force of will, perseverance, compassion, and insight are the qualities that gave him a second opportunity as governor only two short years hence; and they are also the qualities that have led him to become the most powerful political figure in the United States and thereby, the world. For those of us who have had the opportunity to know Bill, and especially those who have worked with him, we can all take pride that we have made some small contribution to his successful journey to the White House.

•   •   •

I had a wonderful personal experience working as chief of staff daily with this vibrant leader. But, he was sometimes exasperating as well. Scheduling was a particular problem as Bill would invite everyone in Arkansas to drop by the Capitol for a visit—and, they would! Then, he would complain to the staff about not having any free time. *Complain* is being generous; sometimes he was out-and-out cranky. After listening to him nag me one day and after reflecting on the problem, Barbara Renas, the governor's secretary, sent me a note saying that the security guards had a man in custody who had come to see the governor so that he could inflict bodily harm on his person. So, I sent the message on to Randy White, the scheduling director, with my own note, which read: "Randy, see if you can work this guy in today."

I Just Went to School in Arkansas

ROY REED

 ne day twenty-two years ago, in 1970, a collected, confident young woman from Illinois walked through the student lounge of Yale University Law School and overheard an accent that sounded out of place. The voice was saying, "Not only that, we have the largest watermelons in the world!"

The young woman asked her companion, "Who *is* that?"

"Oh, that's Bill Clinton," she was told. "He's from Arkansas, and that's all he ever talks about."

A little to her surprise, Hillary Rodham married Bill Clinton. She would see her brash young man become the youngest governor in the country, get himself thrown ingloriously out of office, return in triumph, and finally be elected president of the United States.

The two of them—who were not so much New South as New American—achieved something so subtly brilliant that it has been easily lost on outsiders. Thanks to the Clintons' leadership, the tail-tucked citizens of Arkansas lost a little of their suspicion of the United States. The reason is that their state, largely through the Clintons' energy and genius, finally got tired of bringing up the rear in the field that matters most for self-esteem: Education.

The state that Miss Rodham acquired, for better or worse, with her marriage vows is a wrenching mixture of beauty and squalor. In a day's drive from the delta to the mountains, you can see a million dollars' worth of plows in a single soybean field and, across the state, Hereford cattle grazing in Ozark meadows that a Montana rancher would envy. Without half trying, you can also see ragged children skulking in junkyards. On the rocky back roads, you can still find the whipped and sullen hillfolk of the Arkansas Traveler legend:

> Traveler: How far is it to the next house?
> Squatter: I don't know. I ain't never measured it, and I ain't never
>   been there.
> Traveler: Well, do you know who lives here?
> Squatter: I do.
> Traveler: Then what might your name be?
> Squatter: It might be Tom and it might be Dick, but it lacks a damn
>   sight of either.

The main political problem that Bill Clinton faced when he became governor was a statewide inferiority complex. Arkansas had been crippled by suspicion and defensiveness since the days of wilderness, a century and a half ago. The inhabitants had always believed that their state was doomed to mediocrity or worse; that their children should not set their sights too high, because people from so poor and backward a state could not hope to compete in the larger world; and, most debilitating of all, that Arkansas probably could not be improved because it did not have the money, the brains, the will, the desire, or the need to do so. The place had always been this way; why bother?

It is hard to overstate the power of such inertia and the difficulty of the political problem that it caused. How does a modern leader motivate a people who have never seen themselves as truly part of the American dream? Those who sit in the boardrooms of New York,

Pittsburgh, and Chicago become accustomed to thinking of places like Arkansas (and Alabama, Kentucky, and West Virginia) as merely repositories of resources—oil, minerals, coal, timber. At the other end, the people who live in the repositories get used to the idea that they do not control their own lives. It is an easy step from that colonial mentality to acceptance of last place as a natural condition.

Even educated people in Arkansas dread visiting other places for fear of being revealed as ignoramuses—a fear that outsiders are willing enough to encourage. Miller Williams, the poet, who was born in Arkansas and who taught at the University of Arkansas, says that when he was at the American Academy in Rome in 1977, the first question from strangers was often, "You're from Arkansas? How did you ever win the Prix de Rome?"

Assistant Professor Hillary Rodham first encountered the old Arkansas burden one day in 1975. She had finally given in to Clinton's urging and had joined him as a teacher of law at the University of Arkansas. During a class on criminal law, a young man exasperated her by refusing to focus on the question she was asking.

"I kept after him and after him, and finally he just threw up his hands and said, 'Why don't you leave me alone? What do you expect? I just went to school in Arkansas!'"

From his perspective, that was a rational excuse. He had known all his life that Arkansas ranked forty-ninth or fiftieth in all the measures of educational effectiveness: teacher pay, per-pupil expenditures, percentage of four-year college graduates, curriculum offerings. He probably knew that more than one hundred high schools in the state taught no chemistry or foreign languages. Everybody understood that you could not expect any better from a state that ranked forty-ninth in per-capita income, forty-seventh in factory workers' earnings, and second in poverty. Until World War II, Arkansas had virtually no middle class. It had about one country club—full of rich people and landowners— and two million peasants, sharecroppers, and struggling shopkeepers. Miss Rodham's student had absorbed that knowledge with his mother's milk.

To the young man's surprise, his teacher was not sympathetic.

"I was furious," she said. "I couldn't understand what had

prompted that, and I really was angry. To seek refuge behind this 'poor me, I'm just from Arkansas' mentality was, to me, unacceptable."

Hangdogism did not exist in Park Ridge, Illinois, where she grew up. The children of that affluent suburb of Chicago were reared to believe that America was theirs, and that they could achieve anything they wished. Where Hillary Rodham was a child, the American mainstream was a Mississippi River of opportunity. Young Hillary's high-school teachers were among the best in the nation. She went away to Wellesley and did brilliantly. She went on to Yale law school and did brilliantly again. That was the kind of performance expected of a Park Ridge child.

If Miss Rodham did not understand the Arkansas defensiveness, the man she married did. He knew how lucky he had been to escape it. He might have grown up as Redneck Bill, sulled up like a possum against a stump. His father was an engineer with a job in another state. One weekend as he was driving home to see his young wife, he was killed on the highway in southern Missouri. Bill was born two months later.

The boy spent most of his first four years with his mother's parents. They owned a country store at Hope, which called itself "The Watermelon Capital of the World" but was not known for much else. The boy could easily have become a castoff. But his people cared. His grandmother, against all the odds for that place and time, believed in racial justice. Bill grew up to be an integrationist. She also believed in books. He was reading by the age of three.

"In my family, starting with my grandparents," he would recall, "there was every presumption that I could do anything I wanted to do; that I had the same opportunities that anybody else had, if I worked hard enough. And they set out to make sure that I did work hard enough.

"I knew the poverty of my roots. But my people were optimistic and demanding. I always had a passion about trying to get rid of this 'poor me' attitude a lot of people have about Arkansas, or this sense of limitation, or 'What do you expect—this is just Arkansas, and we can't do this, that, or the other.' I was raised by people who deliberately tried to disabuse me of that idea from the time I was old enough to think."

They succeeded. He went to Georgetown University and did well enough to win a Rhodes scholarship to Oxford. If he was not at the top of his class at Yale law school, he at least managed to marry the class star.

After they graduated from law school, Hillary worked a few months for the Children's Defense Fund (she's still on the board and still interested in the legal rights of children). Then she spent eight months working for John Doar in the House Judiciary Committee's inquiry into the impeachment of President Richard M. Nixon. Bill returned to Arkansas to teach law and run, unsuccessfully, for Congress. He was trying for the House seat once held by J. William Fulbright, also a Rhodes scholar and one of young Clinton's heroes.

Clinton was twenty-eight when he first ran for office. He became known at once as a latter-day New Dealer, lashing out at unrestrained corporate power and warning that big business could end up running the country. When he ran for governor four years later, he dropped that issue in favor of local concerns such as economic development, education, and high utility rates. He won the governor's office in 1978. He was thirty-two.

Political problems began in his first term. As state attorney general a year earlier, he had jumped on rising utility rates as a popular issue. As a young governor, he continued to fight the major electric utility, historically a power in Arkansas politics. But the main problem of his first term was one that few people understood until it was too late. The state's highways needed repairs. He raised car license fees to pay for them, and angered thousands of motorists. They turned him out at the 1980 election. The man who beat him was Frank White, an affable, unimaginative Republican with a blustering style and an aversion to syntax.

"I felt sort of sick," Clinton would recall later, with some understatement. "But the next day I resolved that I was going to run for governor again. I knew at some deep-down emotional level that I would have to run again in 1982 in order to live with myself the rest of my life."

He and Hillary went into seclusion for several months. Then he began to travel. He went to almost every county and, in private meetings, asked his old supporters what he had done wrong. They told him: He had become uppity; people resented his Ivy League style; his staff had been unresponsive. His ego suffered, and he lost some of his cockiness. But people close to him say that he matured. When it came time to run again, he thrashed White.

During the two years the Clintons were out of the governor's mansion, the education issue had moved to the front, not only in Arkansas but across the nation. People everywhere were stirred by national reports on the sorry state of the schools. Most of the Southern states, traditionally the laggards in education, began to raise standards and to increase revenues for better teachers and enriched curricula.

Arkansas, as usual, was bringing up the rear. But Bill and Hillary Clinton were plotting to change that. She still smarted from the "poor me" attitude that she had found in every part of the state.

The reform campaign began slowly. The first legislative session of Clinton's second term in early 1983 produced little more than an Educational Standards Committee.

"Just another study committee," people said.

Then the governor appointed the committee chairman: Hillary Rodham Clinton.

The audacity brought a statewide gasp. Mrs. Clinton had only recently got on the good side of the old-timers. She had alienated many during her husband's first term by keeping her own name. "Hillary Rodham" had cost him votes. In the second race against Frank White she had become "Hillary Rodham Clinton," but some were still cool toward her.

Meanwhile, political pressures were building on all sides. The state Supreme Court handed down a decision in May that made some action necessary. The money for the state's 371 school districts had to be distributed more equitably, the court said. That meant that the legislature and the governor had to write a new state-aid formula, and that probably could not be done without a tax increase.

Clinton had angered the utilities early, and since then had added to his list of enemies the powerful lobbies of the trucking companies, big agriculture, and the timber industry. Their main complaint was a new tax on heavy trucks. They and their friends could be counted on to obstruct anything that the governor wanted.

In addition, many Arkansawyers simply did not believe in spending for education. The average Arkansas teacher earned $14,506 in 1981–82. That was $4,651 below the national average, but it was more than multitudes of ordinary workers earned. In a state where illiteracy was considered to be no more serious than childhood mumps, education was not politically sexy.

The Clintons went to work. During the spring and summer of 1983, the governor took to the podium and urged people to get worried. Without better education, he said, Arkansas would never be ready for the new America of high technology and economic opportunity. It was time to join the mainstream, he said. Above all, he felt for the hidden seed of pride in the hillbilly breast. Every speech contained a sure-fire goad: "Even Mississippi is ahead of us now!"

While he worked the big towns and civic clubs, Hillary worked the back roads. She dragged the fifteen members of the Educational Standards Committee into every corner of the state. They held hearings in drafty lunchrooms. They listened. They asked questions. They made notes. Expense money was short, so they cadged food and lodging. Months later, they were ready with sweeping recommendations—and so was the public, thanks largely to Hillary Clinton and her husband.

To the surprise of people who had not known her well, she had become as effective a speaker as he. She spoke without notes, every sentence perfectly formed. She had also become adept at answering the prickly questions of reporters and the sneers of opponents. People learned to like and trust her.

The legislature met in special session in the fall of 1983. The infighting was long and tough, but when it was over the Clintons had won the lawmakers over, by a thin majority, on some vital bills. Taxes were raised and school aid equalized. Teacher pay was increased by three thousand dollars a year. Small, inefficient school districts were told, in effect, to raise their students' achievements or merge. And fifty districts did merge into larger districts over the next nine years, and to meet the standards most of the others raised local taxes, often by a third or more. Most of all, the state Board of Education adopted the dramatically higher standards recommended by Hillary Clinton's committee.

Arkansas now required smaller class sizes, longer school days, and a longer school year. A high-school student had to take 25 percent more courses than before to get a diploma. More English, mathematics, and science were required, and a student was allowed to fritter away less time with undemanding elective courses. All pupils had to pass tests in basic skills after the third, sixth, and eighth grades. If a school's failure rate was too high, its accreditation could be taken away.

The most disputed new requirement, this one first broached by Hillary and enacted by the legislature, affected teachers. They had to pass competency tests to make sure they had the basic skills needed for teaching.

The Clintons were not unscathed after pushing the program through. In spite of receiving the largest pay raise in the state's history, many teachers were furious at being tested like children. The governor was criticized for not fighting hard enough to increase taxes equitably, and labor leaders were alienated by the governor's failure to achieve, or to push aggressively enough, tax reform. Business lobbies had terrorized enough legislators to kill modest increases in the taxes on corporate income and natural gas that were to make the tax program fair. That left a one-cent rise in the sales tax to pay the whole cost of the $150 million program. In addition, everyone understood that special interests would try to undo many of the reforms when the legislature met again in 1985.

But Clinton kept the program intact the next few years, and the state began to experience the most dramatic improvement in its educational system in generations. Because of that, the Arkansas burden began to lift. The mass inferiority complex had cracked at last.

When he reflected later on how it came about, Clinton joined the crowd and gave credit to his wife. He recalled the day when her role was decided.

"We were sitting around talking about it, and I said, 'This could be the most important thing we'll ever do. Who should I name the chairman of the Standards Committee? The chairman is the key.'

"Either the first or the second day we talked about this—we talk about a lot of things like this—she said, 'I think I'd like to be it. Maybe I'll do it.'"

He reminded her that she had just taken eight months away from her law practice to help him get reelected. She was a partner in one of the most prestigious firms in Little Rock.

"She said, 'Yeah, but this may be the most important thing you ever do, and you have to do it right.'

"Immediately, the minute it was done, I knew it was the right thing to do. I really do believe, as I've said in public many times, that Hillary is the ablest person I've ever known."

Hillary Clinton was not the first northern benefactor that Arkansas has had. Winthrop Rockefeller moved to the state in the 1950s to escape a highly publicized failing marriage and stayed to become governor. He had a large part in mending the racial schism left by the last days of Jim Crow. He invested lavishly in Arkansas business. He lured outside industry. He and his second wife encouraged the arts and uncovered a hidden pool of local talent. He revived the state Republican party.

Unlike Rockefeller, Hillary Clinton had no previous notoriety. No one in Arkansas had heard of her before she moved to the state and married its rising star. Almost no one is aware, for example, that her Park Ridge family was Republican. She campaigned for Barry Goldwater for president when she was sixteen. That might have helped her in conservative Arkansas, where some thought she was too liberal, but she never talked of her origins, or of her political transformation. After Goldwater, she joined the anti–Vietnam-War movement and worked with poor blacks in Roxbury.

How did these two, the privileged northerner and the scrabbling southerner, get together?

It did not happen on that first, inauspicious day. She apparently thought it preposterous that an idler who sat bragging about watermelons would ever interest her. He would not remember seeing her at all that day. He became aware of her months later in a class. He began following her, stumbling and staring, trying to get up his nerve. After two weeks, he encountered her one day in the law library and was so distracted that he could do nothing but stare.

"Finally, she came up to me, just walked up," he said later. "She said, 'If you're going to keep staring at me, I'm going to keep looking back. At least, we ought to know each other's names. I'm Hillary Rodham. What's your name?' I was so stunned I couldn't remember my name. I just tried to get under the bench."

He made it clear from the beginning that he had no interest in a big eastern law firm or in clerking at the Supreme Court. He had one goal. He wanted to go home and run for office.

"He talked about Arkansas all the time," she said. "I never even knew he was a Rhodes scholar for months."

When she finally got him to talk, he went on for three hours about the legal system in the Soviet Union, a subject he had studied at Oxford. He would admit later that he was more interested in Hillary than in Soviet law. He had been stalling.

"I knew it was trouble. I just didn't know whether I wanted to get involved. Hillary was a kind of figure around the law school, a fairly well-known person, you know, and I was not so much because I had seven jobs, and I fooled around with Connecticut politics, besides. I knew that she was highly regarded and all that sort of stuff, and I could tell right away that she had a great career. And I thought, 'Why am I doing this to myself? If I fall in love with this woman, she probably thinks Arkansas is on the other side of the moon. It's just going to be terrible.'

"My wife is the most interesting person I've ever known," Clinton said. And even the old-timers came to share his enthusiasm. The Arkansas Press Association, made up mainly of country editors and publishers, named her "Headliner of the Year" in 1983. The award was to the person who made the most good news for Arkansas.

The Clintons have protected the privacy of their daughter, Chelsea, but their feeling toward her has been no secret. One person saw the governor interrupt an important breakfast meeting to drive Chelsea to school. I saw Mrs. Clinton's calm, composed face melt with adoration one morning at a ballet class. A dozen children were performing for their parents, and her little girl was one of them.

But the two of them together—Bill and Hillary—that is a sight that people would drive miles to see and ponder. They are a little of a puzzle. Their romance is not showy. They do not pet and kiss for the cameras. In public, he calls her Hillary, not Honey. She calls him Bill, not Darling. But they manage to leave no doubt that each is the most important person in the other's life, and that together they are somehow larger than the sum of Bill Clinton and Hillary Rodham.

Hillary Rodham could have made it anywhere—Washington, New York, Chicago. She said there was never any doubt, after she came to know him, that she would move home with Bill Clinton. The reason was simple, she said. His roots were stronger than hers.

"He was from somewhere," she told me. "He wanted to go home there. He knew what he wanted to do there."

She and I were talking in Fayetteville, her favorite Arkansas town, at the home of her old friends James and Diane Blair. The Blairs are important in Arkansas. He is a leading lawyer and industrial executive and a longtime Democratic party leader. She is a political scientist at the University of Arkansas and a strong party worker. But tonight they were just old friends, and they all wore jeans and sat on the floor and ate pizza.

Mrs. Clinton was trying hard, using the force of her intellect, to make me understand why she had chosen to live in Arkansas.

"I had never really been part of any place as rich or as full as this place. Park Ridge, Illinois, was a wonderful place to grow up. It gave me a terrific education, and a superb park system. But it is not the kind of place that I felt rooted to in the way that my husband felt rooted to Arkansas."

I tried to tell her that I understood. She went on.

"I really was excited by what he wanted to do. I knew that he could make a contribution, and a significant contribution. It was exciting."

The Blairs' phone rang. It was Bill, calling from two hundred miles across the state. Hillary walked serenely to the phone. They chatted a few minutes. I don't know what he said to her, but her finely composed face suddenly collapsed, and she stood in the middle of Diane Blair's kitchen and giggled like a schoolgirl.

Lessons from
the Student

PAUL ROOT

School superintendents throughout Arkansas were beseeching Governor Clinton during the summer of 1983 to call a special session of the legislature to raise taxes to help their schools. The Arkansas Supreme Court in the spring had declared that the inequalities among the state's 365 school districts were unconstitutional, and many districts would face huge losses when state funds were reshuffled to equalize school spending. One group of superintendents told Don Ernst and me, both assistants to the governor, of its unhappiness with Clinton for not showing leadership during a time of great need. I explained that the governor was aware of the schools' plight and would call a legislative session as soon as he believed the people of Arkansas would support a tax increase.

"You mean," one of them asked wryly, "he's going to wait until it's *popular* to raise taxes?" Don and I assured them they would not have to wait long. We asked if they had tried to raise taxes locally, which required a vote of the people. They said they had, more than once. For weeks that summer, Bill Clinton was on the road almost every day and night talking about the need to improve education so that Arkansas could attract better jobs and create a better quality of life. He called attention to the state's chronic unemployment, changing work conditions, and the state's need to compete in a world economy. Jobs were leaving for Mexico, Korea, Taiwan, even Bangladesh, and they were not going to return. He said that people who had lost their jobs on the farms to technology were now losing their jobs in the shirt and shoe factories to cheap foreign labor.

The unemployed needed to be retrained, children needed better basic education, and tens of thousands of the adult illiterate needed to be taught to read.

"How many of you," he asked night after night in communities with 7 to 15 percent unemployment rates, "would be willing to lower your own standard of living by paying higher taxes in order to improve education and enhance the lives of all Arkansans in the future?" Four of every five said they would.

A school standards committee, which was chaired by Bill's wife, Hillary, was already at work. The committee began with an inventory of public education and found some astounding things. One hundred ninety-two Arkansas school districts offered no art courses. One hundred eighty-seven offered no music. Seventy-four offered no chemistry. One hundred sixty-seven offered no physics. One hundred eighteen offered no advanced mathematics. Three hundred nine offered no computer science. One hundred sixty-three offered no foreign language.

The University of Arkansas at Fayetteville had published new admission standards requiring freshmen to have taken a foreign language and advanced science and mathematics classes. These standards meant that at least 163 high-school valedictorians would enter their state university on probation if they chose to go there. These were rural and small-town school districts. Larger schools had crowded classrooms, and many elementary schools did not have guidance counselors or librarians.

Hillary's committee held hearings in all seventy-five counties and heard from every curriculum organization and hundreds of parents, teachers, and business leaders. In the end, the committee recommended tough new standards that schools would have to meet by 1987 or else be consolidated with districts that did meet them.

When the standards were completed, Clinton called a special legislative session to raise more money for education and to outline specifically how the schools were to be improved. The major issues for the legislature to consider were taxes, a new formula for distributing state aid among the schools, and the teacher test, which was to be given to administrators as well but which became known as "the teacher test."

Almost daily, Clinton was receiving samples of teachers' poor writing that were sent home with students. Angry parents were forwarding them to the governor's office, and they were saying that they would support taxes for education only if they could see and measure improvements from the taxes. Sam Bratton, another aide of the governor, and Ernst and I met with Clinton at the mansion from six o'clock until far into the night before the session was to begin the next day. About eleven o'clock, Clinton asked our opinion about testing all public school teachers and administrators on their basic skills. Those who couldn't pass the test could not be licensed again when their certifications expired.

I was a first-generation college person from a farm, I explained, and I did not have terrific confidence in my ability to do well on standardized tests. I thought I would pass, but I didn't think my score would reflect my ability to teach. Ernst objected, too. He pointed out that teachers had worked hard to reelect the governor and would feel betrayed by being forced to take a test to keep their careers. Bratton supported the test if it would help persuade legislators to pass the tax increases. A few legislators were already making a teacher test a condition of voting for taxes. Clinton thanked us and said he would have to decide by the next day. He addressed the legislature and the state by television the next night, and he included the test as part of his reforms, although he said his advisors disagreed.

After the legislature passed the testing legislation, the Arkansas

Education Association circulated a newsletter that described the injustice of the test and the possibility of humiliation. The telephone calls to the governor's office became more frequent and less friendly. Ernst and I spent hours each day answering questions from teachers. One morning at a staff meeting, Clinton told us of a call from a teacher whom he knew well and knew to be bright and a good teacher. She was concerned about the test, and he was stunned. After the test was finally given, many teachers said it was too easy, and they were insulted. My wife and son, both teachers, took the test and had no trouble. Since I was trying to convince teachers every day that the test would improve their profession, I decided that I should take it. I was not insulted by its simplicity. Ninety-one percent of the teachers passed all sections of the test the first time they took it, but more than twelve hundred, after several attempts, never passed it.

The special session of the legislature ended after five stormy weeks with a new formula for funding schools; an additional 1 percent sales tax; provisions for the teacher test; a law that required testing of all students at the end of the third, sixth, and eighth grades and that barred them from advancing without passing the eighth-grade test; and a variety of other requirements and incentives for higher school achievement. That winter, the state Board of Education adopted the rigorous curricular standards for the schools written by Hillary's committee. By 1987, thirty-six school districts had failed to meet the standards and had been consolidated. Other local school officials persuaded their constituents to sharply raise local taxes to meet the standards and avoid consolidation—usually after blaming Bill Clinton for the predicament. More than 80 percent of the local tax votes during that three-year period resulted in tax increases.

Some people thought Bill Clinton was inconsistent in his efforts to improve the public schools. He signed a law allowing children to be schooled at home. He had said he believed in choices in education as well as in other areas of life, and he asked me to meet with the advocates of home schooling and to study the options. Having spent ten years working with schools on the problems of desegregation, I went into the process with a bias against home schooling. It was a way, I believed, to avoid going to school with African-American children. In my second meeting with two couples who wanted to teach their children at home, they brought their pastor. They were white; he was black. My theory was ruined. I started to listen. Many parents were already teaching their children at home. They were not asking for a privilege but for protection from prosecutors and overzealous local school officials who wanted to treat them as criminals. The home-school supporters agreed to have their children take nationally standardized tests. I thought, here are people who are willing to assume full responsibility for their children, and we are trying to discourage them. Bill Clinton always was ahead of me on educational issues. He knew the history of public education in the United States, of its original intent to teach children to read the Bible, and he believed in giving parents a wide choice in schooling. His own responsibility was to improve the public schools.

While the state was debating school standards, Clinton was invited to send ten people to a rural education conference in Washington, D.C. He asked me to assemble a team of rural educators. President Ronald Reagan was to be the closing speaker at the conference, but he canceled, and Clinton was asked to take his place. I called the governor's office each day from the conference and outlined the major points made by each of the speakers. In his speech on the final day, the governor mentioned the problems identified by each speaker and explained what we were trying to do about them in Arkansas. He received a standing ovation when he said, "No student in America should be penalized educationally because of where he or she was born." That day in June 1985 was the first time I encountered people from other states asking, "Will Bill Clinton ever run for president?"

Some people were beginning to ask the same thing, but not warmly, back in Arkansas. I entered the office of the superintendent of a rural school, told him I was from Bill Clinton's office, and said I was there to help him. He showed me a mountain of paperwork from the state Education Department that he had to fill out to document his school's compliance with the new standards. "I used to teach a class," he said. "Now I can't keep up with all this useless junk just designed to make Clinton a presidential contender." Student testing, educational standards, and some other reforms could not be realized because they were based on the assumption that students had the ability to improve what they had been doing, the superintendent said. "The governor hasn't been out here where I work," he said. "He doesn't know what the real world is like." It was a recurring theme as I traveled the state visiting with educators: Bill Clinton was too well educated and too far removed from the average Arkansan. But when teachers, administrators, parents, and business people talked about specific reforms, they acknowledged their value. They liked Bill Clinton and they agreed with his changes, but no one had ever proposed this much change in such a short time.

As Bill Clinton's former world-history teacher, I thought I should remind him that the king who introduced too much change in his first year was usually beheaded in his second. Clinton reminded me that we only had until the next election to do whatever we believed needed to be done.

Though I never liked political campaigns, I left the governor's office in 1984 and 1986 to work in his reelection campaigns. I felt inadequate as his stand-in at campaign events. When one is short, overweight, and unknown, the impact is less than desirable. I represented him at a small town in north central Arkansas, where I shared the platform with twenty-eight county politicians and several country-music groups. I sent Bill a note saying that I had spoken for him between "I Stopped Loving Her Today" and "Can I Lean on You, Leona?"

I also stood in for him at Toad Suck Daze, a festival in Conway. I had memorized a five-minute speech recounting Bill's accomplishments, but they told me to forget the speech and race the governor's frog, which had been picked for him. If your frog won on Saturday, you raced him again in the finals on Sunday. Part of my rearing was in a rural Baptist church between Bald Knob and Augusta, and while there were instructions in the Bible that I still didn't understand, I was pretty clear on the moral implications of racing frogs on the Sabbath. When the whistle blew, I held the right leg of the Clinton frog, ensuring that he would race at a forty-five-degree angle and be disqualified. I do not know for sure what Bill Clinton would have done, but I know that my Sunday School teacher at the Worden Baptist Church would have been proud of me.

Improving relations between the government and church groups was one of the most enjoyable tasks assigned to me by Clinton. He and I met once with a small group of preachers who had visited a preacher in Nebraska who was in jail for running a religious day-care center in violation of state law. All day-care teachers had to be certified by the state, and the preacher had defied the law. While Arkansas had no such law, it did require child centers to provide a certain amount of space per student, food, fire protection, and copies of immunization records. The preachers saw the requirements as an encroachment on their ministry. Others said the state had to guarantee the safety of preschool children. Obviously, we had conflicting beliefs. Clinton appointed several of these people to a committee to work out something that would be acceptable to both sides. The agreement was that the churches could be exempt from state certification. The legislature passed the bill, and the governor signed it. Two weeks later, it was challenged in court as unequal treatment of children. We were still searching for a compromise.

Bill enjoyed a good relationship with many church groups. He attended a church camp in the Redfield community each summer and often sang there with a quartet of pastors. Seeing their governor singing "Amazing Grace" with four of their beloved pastors was inspiring, many of them told me. They had never had any relationship with a governor before. He brought other people closer to government. On one Saturday every May while Clinton was governor, the vale-dictorians and salutatorians from every high school in Arkansas were invited to the governor's mansion with their families. A band played in the back yard, food and soft drinks were served in tents, pictures were taken, and then all the students and their parents entered the mansion to shake hands, talk, and have their pictures taken with Bill and Hillary—more than seven hundred pictures were taken in one afternoon.

You can throw a dart at a map of Arkansas and no matter where it lands Bill Clinton will start naming people who live there and will tell you what wonderful folks they are and the last time he had supper with them. More people know and feel close to Bill Clinton than to any other politician in Arkansas history. Yes, he has high negatives because he has asked people to take responsibility for solving age-old problems. Everyone wanted better highways, schools, and health care, but some people never made the connection between services and taxes.

Bill Clinton was a student in my advanced world-history class at Hot Springs High School when he was fifteen. All the students in that class were very good. The difference was Bill's depth of enjoyment of history. Even at that age, he was talking about working in the foreign service.

I saw Bill from time to time over the next two decades. Two years after the world-history class and after completing my doctorate and teaching at Ouachita Baptist University, I returned to Hot Springs to fill in as choir director at the Park Place Baptist Church, his church. Bill came up to say hello at the end of the Sunday night service. We went to a coffee shop and talked. I realized then how bright he really was and how he had grown in understanding. In that coffee shop in 1964, our roles reversed. He was becoming the teacher and I the student.

The reversal was completed in January 1983, when I became a special assistant to the governor. The voters had returned him to office after a two-year exile, and the legislature was in session. We met each morning at 7:15 until legislative committees started meeting. I was amazed at the breadth and depth of issues that were covered. I would tell Bill everything I knew about the bills that were to be taken up by the education committees of the Senate and House of Representatives, and Don Ernst would speak on behalf of the teachers. Bill would end the session by teaching us a lesson in school finance. Then the discussion would turn to the issues before all the other legislative committees that day. He would know about every bill, every issue, whom it would affect, and who would be against the bill. I wondered how anyone could learn that much that fast. But he would always consider the people who were not at the meeting. "Whom will it affect?" he would ask about legislation. "Will it affect people who aren't represented up here?" I would sometimes object to criticism of him that seemed unreasonable. He said people felt left out of the decision-making process and that most of them never went to the capitol to let their feelings be known. He said he heard their frustrations when he campaigned every two years. "I owe them respect and some of my time," he would say. "If I can solve their problem without creating a greater problem for others, it's my duty to try."

His Finest Hour*

PAUL GREENBERG

Whatever its historic accomplishments (in education) or its historic failures (in equity), the special session of the legislature in October and well into November of 1983 produced something even more important than a program of education. Perhaps not since Winthrop Rockefeller has a governor of Arkansas so challenged the legislature to overcome its ingrained inertia and rise above its usual self. Tax laws and state standards can be changed every session of the legislature; the opportunity to develop a great governor doesn't occur as regularly.

This special session of the legislature seemed almost as long as the regular one. For almost six weeks, Bill Clinton faced down a long line of special interests, whether they came wrapped in mercantile respectability, or pseudo-academic pretension. The state Chamber of Commerce, the Arkansas Poultry Federation, the Arkansas

*This article appeared originally in *Arkansas Times* in February 1984.

(not so) Educational Association—the governor took them on one after the other, or all at once, whatever was their pleasure, like Douglas Fairbanks whirling his way through a swashbuckler.

Clinton didn't have to do all that. He could have made some cosmetic compromises, proclaimed them all Great Reforms, and gone home. Then he wouldn't have antagonized corporations that net over a hundred thousand dollars a year or those teachers and school administrators who disapprove of tests, at least for themselves. He could have appeased the chicken lobby, the beer-and-wine people, and other special interests. But it was as if he had set out to offend all of his old political allies except the people, as if he had decided to do right and simply trust the public. Whether that will help or hurt him politically, the governor should be able to sleep soundly of nights after this special session. And after this Extraordinary Session of the General Assembly—the longest since they've been keeping records—he probably needs to.

No, the governor didn't win them all. But he tried to. He cut to the heart of issues, he compromised where he felt he had to, he fought the good fight, and he let some other folks know they had been in one. He threatened to kill his entire tax program, on which he had staked his all this special session, unless it was accompanied by higher standards for education. At one point or another during the session, he took on greed and apathy and ignorance and arrogance—not to mention some hurtful, gratuitous distortions directed against him, his program, and his wife. (The Arkansas Education Association, once such a fine organization, has seldom looked so low.) In short, he acted like a public servant—and a magnificent fighter.

This was a new Bill Clinton, and let's hope he sticks around. It wasn't Slick Willie, the governor who dominated the regular, do-nothing session of the legislature. Slick Willie was almost invisible at the special session. This time the governor acted like a governor. He rose above his old campaign rhetoric about not supporting a tax raise (no matter how badly Arkansas might need one) and boldly proposed several. He ignored the windy warnings—they sounded more like threats—that meeting the challenge this state faces in education would mean the end of his political career. That may have been the right appeal to win over Slick Willie, but not this Bill Clinton.

The governor did his homework and spade work this time. He didn't scatter his efforts. He concentrated on one subject—education—the one most likely to shape the state's future. And in that one field, he proposed a comprehensive program of reform: a better distribution of state aid designed to eliminate those expensive phantom students and provide a more equal education for the real ones; new taxes to finance this revolution and to make certain that bad schools weren't improved at the expense of good ones; and new, higher standards for education. The taxpayers weren't just asked to put up more money; they were assured that their money wouldn't be wasted.

Clinton proved ready to compromise on what was less than essential during this session, but not on principle. It was invigorating to watch him face down the Arkansas Education Association, an organization that was once a beacon of light in this state when Forrest Rozzell led it but that is fast becoming just another blinkered special interest. The governor seemed to know when to give a little, and when not to give a fraction of a millimeter.

Clinton could have pursued the bubble popularity once again; that would not have surprised cynics and others who have watched Slick Willie get the better of him on too many occasions. That didn't happen this time. The governor got a lot more of the substance than Slick Willie would have settled for, and less of the shine. Faced with a court order and a chronic problem that had become an acute crisis after decades of neglect, Clinton turned that crisis into opportunity—opportunity seized.

The future of education, and not the outcome of the next election, dominated the special session. Surely that is the way the people of Arkansas wanted it. But the people don't always get what they want, or what the state needs, when the legislature goes into session and the state into fear. This time, the General Assembly closed on a note of hope and accomplishment.

One big reason for that happy ending was Bill Clinton's leadership. To quote a plain-spoken, independent-minded legislator, Representative Charles Moore of Luxora: "I've never been a big fan

of Bill Clinton . . . In the last few weeks, he has gained my admiration." Moore may be talking for lots of folks who have learned to eye
the governor warily over the years, watching all that promise and talent at the service of all that ambition.

This time, Arkansas's governor seemed ambitious most of all for
the state. The special session may be remembered not just for what
it did for the schools, but as the time Bill Clinton came of age as a
political leader. It's not necessarily elections that test a governor, but
what he does afterward, and in between. After this special session, it
was time to retire that pacifier Bill Clinton used to wear in political
cartoons.

The downer didn't come till the last week of the special session,
when it proved to be not too special at all. Then it was business as
usual, with the emphasis on business. The legislature approved a
decent educational program, but it wasn't about to finance it decently.
While raising the ordinary consumer's sales tax from three to four
cents on the dollar, it wouldn't raise the tax on the state's richest corporations, or the state's scandalously low severance tax on natural gas,
or provide a rebate on the sales tax for the poor, or even extend the
sales tax to country-club fees. Despite the governor's pleas for a little
fairness—and that's all he dared ask for, a little—the Ledge wouldn't
budge. It seemed to recognize only one way to raise revenue: Soak the
poor.

It should not be assumed that the entire legislature is composed of
regressives. There are many proud exceptions to the dismal rule in the
Ledge. William F. Foster of England was one of them. This session of
the legislature may have been his finest hour. Representative Foster's
finest minute may have come when he berated his colleagues for their
refusal to increase the corporate income tax slightly (from 6 to 7 percent on corporations with incomes of more than a hundred thousand
dollars a year) and after having raised the sales tax on consumers in
general by a third—from 3 to 4 percent. He had the candor to call this
shame and disgrace "a shame and a disgrace."

Foster was equally plain-spoken about what the legislature had
become in its last week: "a special session for the special interests."

When his plea on behalf of the state's poor and near-poor was met with laughter, he turned to the source and replied: "You can laugh about this if you want to, but you've hurt 99 percent of the people in your district and you're protecting 1 percent."

Another of the governor's proposals—to collect the sales tax on cable television—didn't even make it out of the House Revenue and Taxation Committee. There went another million dollars a year for education. "It seems strange and unbelievable to me," said Representative Jon Fitch of Hindsville, "that we will have a tax on [utilities like] propane and butane, but this luxury in life is not taxed."

But to those who follow the legislature—a habit that requires a strong stomach at times—it's not strange at all; it's all too believable. The interests don't mind improving the state's schools—so long as it is done without goring their pet ox. This well-trained legislature, responding to its master's voice, seemed able to pass only regressive taxes. Result: the people now pay 4 percent on their bread, nothing on their cable TV. Given its sublime sense of fairness, the Arkansas legislature also decided that neither rich nor poor would have to pay sales taxes on their country-club charges.

The governor's final speech to a joint session of the General Assembly wasn't a cry of victory or a complaint against defeat so much as a simple message: Wait Till Next Year. He told the legislature that his education program, which the whole state can take pride in, is "just a beginning, not an end to the work we must do." He brought up the corporate income tax that the legislators had turned down and their failure to raise the state's abysmally low severance tax on natural gas. "I am confident," he said, "that Arkansas will not forever be the only state that gives away its natural resources." It was as if he were making a list for next time. "This is not the end of our efforts in this area," he promised. This boy may have just begun to fight. Correction: This man may have just begun to fight. He is keeping faith with those who elected him to this state's highest office. Their decision has never looked better. And neither has Arkansas's future. The pleasing jangle that the more imaginative could hear when Clinton walked away from the podium after his final words to this special session of the legislature was the sound of the spurs he had just earned.

If anyone deserves more credit than Clinton for awakening Arkansas to the needs of its young people, it may be Mrs. Clinton. As chairman of the statewide committee on standards in education, Hillary Rodham Clinton helped educate a whole state, not excluding her husband. If Clinton has shown a new political maturity this fall, it wouldn't be the first time that the key to a man's growing up would prove to be a woman.

Everyone Will
Do the Right Thing

BOBBY ROBERTS

When I picked up the ringing telephone, Bill Clinton was on the line. After a short chat, he got to the point. We were less than a week away from the 1983 session of the Arkansas legislature, and he wondered if I could get a sixty-day leave of absence from the University of Arkansas at Little Rock to be one of his liaisons with the legislature. Damn, I thought, time has no meaning to him. I should have learned that while trying to keep him on schedule during the recent campaign in which he had regained the office that he had lost in 1980. I would need time both to wrap up my business at the university and to persuade the university's administration to release me to the governor's office. Still, I had hoped that the call would come because, after working as a travel aide during the campaign, I had become addicted to politics. The glacial pace of academia, where I had spent most of my life, now seemed boring.

"I'll do it," I said. "Fine," he replied, and hung up. Clinton undoubtedly returned to the stack of phone calls he needed to make, and I was left to wonder exactly what I had agreed to do. My knowledge of the legislative process had been imparted in my ninth-grade civics class.

Most governors find legislative sessions distasteful because they must put their political future in the hands of other politicians whose concerns and goals often conflict with those of the governors and with those of fellow legislators. The mix of interests in a legislature is always staggering, sometimes irreconcilable, and occasionally explosive. It is into this uncertain political brew that a governor dumps his program, which may result in disaster for him if it is not handled properly. This uncertainty disturbs most governors, but Clinton never feared the process.

Faced with such a chaotic and dangerous political situation, governors can do one of two things to get their programs enacted. They can wield the power of the executive office to crush their enemies and reward supporters, or they can negotiate a settlement that a majority of the general assembly will accept.

In Arkansas, the power tactic is hard to employ because the office of the governor is systemically weak, a circumstance rooted in the post–Civil War era. Reconstruction government in Arkansas was controlled from the governor's office, and when the Democrats finally overthrew the Republican regime, the state ratified the "Redeemer" Constitution, which gutted gubernatorial power and diffused executive responsibility. Real political power passed to the general assembly. Despite recent reforms that strengthened the governor, the office remains a weak instrument compared with that of most other states. The governor still has no direct control of the highway and transportation departments, higher education, the prisons, or the state fish and wildlife commission. Powerful independent management boards run them. The legislature uses interim committees to inject itself into such executive matters as budget transfers, state contracts, and personnel matters within the executive branch. Thus, the doctrine of separation of powers as it is generally practiced in the United States does not exist in Arkansas. The executive department has evolved into a bastardized institution in which the governor, the general assembly, and independent management boards share administrative power. Any governor who seeks to assert much independent executive authority is headed for trouble with the legislature.

Bill Clinton already understood these limitations when he took office a second time in the winter of 1983, and he rarely tried to use power to gain an objective. He preferred to negotiate with the general assembly. Negotiation rather than muscle also is an impulse of Clinton's character. Though he is extremely competitive and takes great pleasure in winning, he finds no satisfaction in defeating opponents.

Politics and public policy to Clinton have a linear relationship. At one end of the line are popular political choices that disregard public-policy questions. At the other end are ideal public policies in which political consequences are ignored. Clinton never seemed to be comfortable with either extreme because he thought that somewhere along the continuum was a place where acceptable public policy merged with political realities. He always searched for that point and seemed to have an intuitive knowledge of where it was.

On rare occasions, the line bent like a horseshoe, the two ideal concepts almost came together, and the best public policy and the political popularity almost matched. It occurred only once in the years that I served Clinton as a legislative assistant. It came in the fall of 1983 at a special session of the legislature when the governor pushed through sweeping educational reforms. That six-week session became the instrument of Clinton's political ascendancy in Arkansas and the nation. Arkansas people began to understand that improving their institutions was both possible and necessary. It made winners of the governor, the legislature, and the people.

My debut as a lobbyist for Bill Clinton was inauspicious. Clinton told me to run down to the Senate Judiciary Committee and ask the chairman, Senator Max Howell, if he would move one of the governor's bills to the top of the morning agenda of his committee. It was a harmless request that no reasonable person would decline, I thought. Howell, who was serving in the legislature when Bill Clinton and I were born, had a reputation for being brusque, but he seemed amiable enough when I knelt beside his chair and introduced myself.

"Bill would like to know if you would mind moving one of his administration bills to the top of the agenda," I said.

"Who wants a bill moved up?" the suddenly red-faced senator roared. "Huh uh, son. You mean *Governor* Clinton. That's what I call him."

"Yes, sir, that's what I mean," I said. "Governor Clinton would like to know if you would move the bill forward."

"I've always done everything I could for that young man, and I'll do anything I can for him," he said.

"Then I can tell Governor Clinton that you'll move the bill to the top of the agenda?" I asked.

"No!" he retorted.

I retreated to the governor's office wondering what I had gotten myself into and how I had managed to torpedo part of his program the first day. Instead of being mad, Clinton laughed throughout my story. Howell had a change of heart, and later he even allowed me to sit quietly in the back of the chamber when the senate was in session. Eventually, several senators, especially Jerry Bookout of Jonesboro and Morriss Henry of Fayetteville, took pity and educated me on the mysteries of the legislature. I learned enough to survive and to realize that the legislature did not deserve the scorn often heaped on it by the Arkansas media.

The 1983 session gave me a chance to observe how Clinton approached the legislative process. It was little different from the way he campaigned. I had learned three things about Clinton when I traveled with him in the 1982 race.

First, his energy is almost limitless. He drove his staff to the point of exhaustion. Our days usually began at dawn and ended at midnight or later. I learned to eat when I could, and my diet consisted almost wholly of catfish, fried chicken, and spaghetti. We were always over-scheduled, but Clinton loved unplanned detours. He would stop at a remote crossroads store and visit at length with whomever he found. Every three or four days, his travel aides wore out and were recycled back to Little Rock. But Clinton drew strength from the crowds and continued the relentless schedule seven days a week.

Second, Clinton had an encyclopedic knowledge and a computer memory. He read prodigiously, even during the campaign, and his mind was crammed with minutiae. He would launch into a mind-numbing stream of facts, figures, and conclusions on any subject anyone brought up.

Third, he was willing to talk to anyone he met. "Stop at that grocery store," he would yell as we sped toward our next appointment. "Bill," I would say, "we are already late. We don't have time." He'd say, "Stop anyway." Soon he would be introducing himself to everyone in the store, and he would wind up in a long and earnest dialogue with a logger who had stopped for some tobacco and who might have a long-held grievance against some level of government. Clinton often would turn to an aide and tell him to follow up on some point. It played havoc with the schedule and made it impossible for Clinton ever to be on time. I at first assumed that Clinton tolerated such long distractions because he disliked being rude or running off even one potential vote. I came eventually to the understanding that these endlessly recurring exchanges about mundane affairs did not have a selfish political motive. Rather, Clinton was genuinely interested in people's problems and what they had to say even if they had ideas that made no practical sense. His concern was rarely lost on the people with whom he spoke.

His perpetual search for these encounters with ordinary people did have an important political consequence. A difficult problem for any elected official is to get information and to discern attitudes that have not been filtered through polls, policy papers, articles, books, expert advisors, and self-serving individuals. Clinton never completely trusted these sanitized sources. He had learned that the problems, desires, and ideas of average people needed to be thrown into the mix. These random exchanges served as sounding boards for Clinton to test his ideas and to learn what people really thought. He would ask a factory worker whether he thought a school curriculum proposal would work. The ability to get in sync with the everyday rhythms of life kept him from moving down policy paths that were political dead ends. The encounters accelerated his learning curve about issues and permitted him to leaven theory and bureaucratic information with reality. The ability to combine ideas with practical experience is his basic political strength. It defines him as a politician.

If President Clinton roams the countryside on a bus, goes on talk shows, talks with people on his jogs or his respites at McDonald's, or if he takes a few seconds to autograph a napkin, he is searching for personal feedback. Without it, his political antennae become blunted. Unfortunately, the system he has now entered discourages such informal meetings. If Clinton cannot find some way to break through the throngs of Secret Service agents, advisors, and media people that engulf his every move, he will lose his most valuable political skill. Clinton is extraordinarily persistent; he may find a way to break out of the presidential cocoon.

I began to see in 1983 how his capacity for work, his encyclopedic knowledge, and his ability to listen and to modify his own notions intersected with the process of making laws. His legislative team's work began at 7:30 each morning in a small room on the northwest corner of the governor's suite in the Capitol, where the governor assessed the progress of all legislation and planned the strategy for the day. Papers and files were scattered around the battered desks that staffers occupied later in the day. An old table and a dozen wooden chairs stood in the middle of the room. The legislative liaisons, the governor's chief aides, Betsey Wright and Maurice Smith, and a smattering of others gathered, along with Clinton. Straggling in by eight o'clock were staff members assigned to certain committees, the press secretary, the director of finance and administration, the head of the revenue department, the governor's legal counsel, and others. The crowd numbered more than thirty, and they sat on the floor, desks, window sills, and the hearth of an old fireplace.

Each bill that was introduced was assigned a grade. Administration bills were given an "A." We spent most of our time shepherding them through the legislature. "B" bills were legislators' bills that we favored and that his liaisons were to push. Most measures were graded "C," which meant that Clinton had no particular position on them, although he sometimes instructed us to help a legislator on a bill. "D" was assigned to bills that we opposed but were likely to die without our interference. "F" bills, ordinarily the smallest group, were live initiatives that Clinton wanted us to fight.

Clinton started down each committee agenda and reviewed the status of each bill.

"Why is our bill on fair teacher dismissal still hung up in committee?" he would ask. "We need to get moving on this. Chris, catch Buddy Turner [chairman of the House Education Committee] before the committee meets and find out what's going on. If you can't get anywhere with Buddy, ask him to come down here and I'll talk to him."

"I saw Buddy Blair last night," he would continue, "and I found out what he is trying to accomplish with HB 1146. I still don't think it will solve his problem, but I don't see how we can oppose it. Let's upgrade it from 'D' to 'C'. Anybody disagree?"

All the bills that we were watching got at least a cursory reexamination each day. Clinton would ask aides who were responsible for categories of bills to explain all the new measures that were introduced the day before and to give an opinion. Sometimes, the discussions turned into free-wheeling debates. Most of us knew that Clinton didn't mind our strenuously disagreeing with him. Out of the give-and-take a consensus was reached. The meetings ended when the ten o'clock committee meetings began, and the liaisons went off to buttonhole legislators whom Clinton wanted to visit with and to gather intelligence from legislators and lobbyists that would help Clinton form a sense of the temper of the assembly. After both houses adjourned each day, some of us met with Clinton to identify the people he needed to talk to that evening to move key legislation along. He left the meetings with long lists of legislators whom he would talk to by telephone often until past midnight, while the rest of us retired to the watering holes around the city where legislators and lobbyists hung out.

After only a few weeks, the long hours and mental stress wore most of us out. Almost everyone on the staff but Clinton wished the legislature would go home and leave us alone. Clinton thrived on it. He loved the probing combat between his own broad agenda and the narrow interests of individual legislators. He would meet with any legislators who wanted a favor from him or who had a bill that they wanted the governor to support. Usually, members' interests had little to do with our program, and Clinton would listen and probe for some common ground for agreement. Even if they didn't agree, they usually parted on friendly terms.

Those of us who had been battling the lobbyists and legislators for his program usually were not pleased with his approach. "Governor," I would say, "this guy wants money for a project in his district. It's vital to his political survival. Let's hold the appropriation bill until he comes around on our bill." Clinton would explain that he understood the senator's position even if he did not agree with it and that he wasn't ready to apply that kind of pressure. He never was. I would sulk, wondering how we would ever pass anything if we did not apply the scant power we had.

Unlike most chief executives, who dislike committee meetings and legislative plenary sessions, Clinton lobbied openly for his programs. He could be found almost every day standing outside a committee room with a cup of coffee in one hand. There he would buttonhole legislators to ask for their help, or he would go into a committee room and kneel beside legislators to talk about an approaching vote, or he would ask for recognition to respond to a witness who had raised points against a bill in which he was interested. Nearly all of his aides tried repeatedly to convince him that such tactics were unwise because he needed to remain aloof from the trench-fighting that went on in the halls of the Capitol and that it was unseemly for a governor to lower himself to common lobbying. He could never restrain himself, and I must acknowledge that he often was able to swing crucial votes in that way without getting committed to doing something he did not want to do.

In his mind, the lawmaking process was like an intellectual game board on which all the players should be willing to sacrifice a few pieces so that they could advance their own positions. His objective was not to give up anything that would ultimately cause him to lose either his political or policy goals. The game had serious consequences for both his own ambitions and for the people of Arkansas. He was always acutely aware of both.

I worked for Clinton in a half-dozen such legislative sessions. The last was a short affair of four days during the early stage of his presidential campaign in February 1992. It was no different. We met early, reviewed our bills, and lobbied to get them passed. Though distracted by the presidential campaign, Clinton negotiated a settlement with the legislature on a complicated package of child-welfare benefits and other issues.

During a decade of association with Clinton, I also served briefly as his liaison with the criminal justice system and was appointed by him to the Arkansas Board of Correction, which oversees the prisons. I rarely was a bearer of good news. I found myself having to tell him something he didn't enjoy hearing. I decided that the best approach was to relate the facts and to advise him on what I thought was the best course, no matter how distasteful it might be. This sometimes led to clashes, and more than once Clinton confused the messenger with the disagreeable message. I never felt intimidated by the exchanges. I always left feeling that he had treated my opinions fairly and that my credibility was intact. I knew that the next time that I had to present him with disagreeable information, I would get a fair hearing. It was not a bad relationship for either of us.

My service with the Clinton administration was not always happy. At times, I became infuriated with his unwillingness either to make difficult decisions quickly or to punish political enemies who thwarted policies that would be good for the state. His inclination was always to be fair and to act honorably. If he sometimes failed my narrow expectations of what ought to be done, it was because he alone had to balance the broader interests of the people with political reality. I did not have to carry that burden.

Despite the political treachery and broken promises that Bill Clinton encountered, he remained astonishingly optimistic about everyone's motives, and he persisted in thinking that anyone could be persuaded to do the right thing. That basic belief in the goodness of people and their inclination to do right is what we should expect from our leaders. We should never expect anything less.

Just Tell Your Story to Me

PHYLLIS ANDERSON

The apple disappeared rapidly, in big bites, starting with the deep crimson skin, then the firm meat, and finally the hard, seedy core, into the mouth and down the throat of Bill Clinton, who then carefully deposited the tiny stem into the wastebasket by his desk. A few senior staff members were gathered around the governor's desk discussing a policy issue while he read and signed a pile of letters—and ate his apple. I have forgotten the issue. I was transfixed by the methodical and efficient consumption of the apple, having always thought that the core of a fruit was unappetizing, if not inedible, and knowing anyway that its eating required the conscious attention of at least some part of the mind. Although I have sat through many such sessions since then, the image of the apple being consumed to the stem amid so much mental activity has stayed with me. It became a metaphor for the way Bill Clinton gobbled up, digested, assimilated, and stored in his memory so much information on so many topics.

Those of us who worked for Clinton learned quickly that, unless our memories matched his, we had better have a good filing system. A senior aide who had written a memorandum to Clinton on a complicated issue was stunned one day after being summoned by the governor to his office. "Remember that memo that you did a few months ago on this issue?" he asked. "You *did* say that by 1991 we would have more than two thousand cases, which would bring our budget to [some amount], didn't you?" The aide replied, "Governor, I'll check on it for you," then left Clinton's office to scramble through his files to retrieve the memorandum and see what he had written. Sure enough, Clinton's figures were precisely right. It happened many times. Even with a staff of bright people who were quick studies in their specialties, Clinton set the standard. All of us who worked there marveled at his ability to juggle many issues and remember large concepts and minute details on almost any topic. None of us had known anyone who could match it. His memory wasn't perfect, but it was extraordinary.

I spent *ten* years working in various capacities for Bill Clinton, and I had initially intended to work for him a couple of years, just long enough to satisfy my curiosity about how state government functioned from the perspective of the office of the chief executive. Although I had spent almost two years after his defeat in 1980 interviewing him and writing a book about his first term, I really did not know Bill Clinton very well. After two weeks on his staff, I began to see the complex and brilliant man for whom I would continue to work for many years.

I stayed for two reasons. It became clear that Clinton was committed to making the lives of Arkansans better and that by helping him, I, too, was doing something worthwhile. Also, every day presented a new intellectual challenge. It became harder and harder to imagine another job that would open up so many worlds of challenging work.

Clinton almost always thought about what needed to be done earlier than most people in public office. One day in the early 1980s, he called me into his office and said that Arkansas needed a statewide adult literacy program. He wanted me to get on it right away. As I walked back to my office, I kept thinking, "Literacy? Literacy? Why literacy? Why now?" I gathered information, talked to people, and finally presented Clinton with a plan of action. As always, he modified it, and we went to work putting it into place. A couple of years later, governors from all over the country were doing the same sort of thing, and Arkansas's plan became something of a model. Time after time, Clinton was ahead of the rest in recognizing problems and doing something about them. He was always out talking to people at the crossroads, factory gates, and executive suites, and he learned what their problems were. He had figured out that illiteracy was a tremendous drag on the economy and on the state's and nation's competitiveness as well as a deterrent to the happiness and prosperity of hundreds of thousands of people.

Clinton's staff members did argue about how to get things done. I have a vivid recollection of sitting in Clinton's office and arguing passionately with another staff member about how to go about solving a particular problem. We argued heatedly for ten minutes before I remembered that we were in Clinton's office. I glanced at him. He was leaning over his desk, absorbed in the argument as if he were watching the closing seconds of an exciting basketball game. We continued making our cases, and, when we had nothing else to say, we looked at Clinton. He put his arms on his desk and reiterated the best points of each argument and then proceeded to tell us how he wanted the issue settled. The solution was a mixture of both arguments but with the usual innovative Clinton stamp. When we stood to leave, all three of us were smiling. Clinton loved that kind of exchange.

H. G. Wells wrote that "No passion in the world is equal to the passion to alter someone else's draft." Clinton evidenced the wisdom of this passion. I usually edited his transcribed speeches so that they would read well to someone who had not been present when he gave the speech. During the ten years that I worked for him, Clinton only spoke from prepared remarks a few times. His practice was to read the briefing notes prepared by the staff, jot down a hasty sketch of the main points he wanted to make (usually while eating at the head table), then stand up and talk for twenty or thirty minutes. We taped and transcribed the speeches; I did the first edits and then gave them to Clinton to edit before they were distributed. He loved to edit other people's drafts and his own remarks, polishing and clarifying them so that they would be fully understandable.

Clinton developed what I think was a unique strategy for educating people, whether they were legislators, fellow governors, or constituents, about real problems and how they could be solved. He first tried this strategy with other governors at a meeting of the National Governors' Association in Washington, D.C. We gathered a few Arkansas people who had been involved in literacy programs or who had made the break from welfare dependency to work. It was daunting for some of those who were called upon because a few of them had never even been to Little Rock, much less to the nation's capital. So it wasn't surprising that when one of the first speakers began to tell why she and her children were happier since she had left welfare and had gone to work, she faltered and couldn't go on. After only a few seconds, during which an uncomfortable silence filled the room (I was holding my breath), Clinton leaned into the microphone, looked directly at her, and asked if she was nervous. She said she was *very* nervous. He said he understood that because the room was full of governors, staff members, and television lights.

"Why don't you just tell your story to me?" he said softly. She did, and there was not a dry eye in the room. Everyone there "got it" in a way that they never would have from the dry discourse of a policy expert. Clinton's sensitivity to the woman and his ability to put her at ease made the session memorable. He often asked citizens to come to legislative hearings and conferences to see firsthand the problems that other people faced.

Clinton's staff was his extended family. He was concerned when we were sick or when tragedy struck our lives. He telephoned me the night my mother died. I was grateful that someone who cared had called, had shared my grief, and had offered some thoughts about coping with the days and months ahead. Two years later, he still asks how I am doing. He knows how long it takes to learn to live with the loss of someone you love.

Clinton's energy is legendary among friends and those who have worked for him, in government or in campaigns. In May of 1988 I traveled with him and two other aides to Hope, Arkansas, where he gave a speech on literacy to L.A. LAW (Lower Arkansas Literacy Awareness Week). It was a last-minute scheduling decision because he had attended Chelsea's ballgame that day, too. Optional appointments were on the schedule, but it was dusk and the aides were tired and ready to go home. Clinton, however, wanted to stop at his boyhood home in Hot Springs. So we stopped while he went inside to meet the family who currently lived there. Having gained a fresh burst of energy from talking with the family, he decided to visit an uncle nearby. The state trooper, the pilot, and I chose to stay in the car and sleep while we could, because we had a premonition that the evening was only beginning. Sure enough, Clinton bounded out of the house an hour or so later, jumped into the car, and told the driver that he wanted to go to a fish fry at a duck-hunting lodge in Washington, Arkansas, some ninety miles southwest of Hot Springs. I asked him why he wanted to go— after all, attending the fish fry was optional, it was late, and the party probably would be over. Nevertheless, we drove to Washington and found the hunting lodge. It was locked and dark inside and plainly empty. Clinton got out of the car, peered into the windows, and walked around the place to make sure that everyone was gone. When he returned to the car, he said, "Be sure to call the sheriff tomorrow and tell him that I came to the fish fry but that everyone had left." I called the sheriff and described the governor's travels the night before. The sheriff felt bad that no one was there.

After another long day of travel, we got into the plane to fly back to Little Rock. I couldn't wait to crawl into my seat and read. But Clinton and two others began a game of hearts, a card game that he loves, and he decided that I should not be left out. I told him that I was not a card player and had never played hearts. "Come on, I'll teach you," he said. He enjoyed teaching someone a new game. When we landed, he said, "Aren't you glad you learned how to play hearts?" Clinton is enthusiastic about whatever he does, whether it is discussing international trade or playing a game of hearts.

Clinton, who always finds one more person to talk to or another child's baseball to sign, was usually late to scheduled appointments.

Every once in a while, however, he was early. I was supposed to fly with him to northwest Arkansas to provide information for a meeting. We were to leave from Central Flying Service at two o'clock on a Sunday afternoon. I left for the airport ten minutes before departure time, thinking that I would get there long before Clinton did. I parked my car, and as I walked into the terminal, I saw a small plane taxi down the runway. I rushed in and asked if it was Clinton's plane. They radioed the plane that I had arrived as it was lifting off, but Clinton's message came back, "Tell her we'll catch her next time." Catch me *next* time? I found a telephone and called a couple of people to see if I should drive to northwest Arkansas since it was an important meeting. I was advised not to go because the meeting probably would be over when I arrived. The next day, Clinton briefed me on the meeting. "See," he said, "I'm not always late!"

Everyone on the governor's staff worked as a team. Clinton put few limits on those who worked for him. If we wanted to try to do something a new way or to move a program in a new direction, he was usually agreeable. He told us that we must take risks to move forward. The saddest people he knew, Clinton said, were those who had dreams but never tried to fulfill them.

Did I ever burn out? Yes. It was in 1987. The pace of work, the volume of letters, the phone calls, the meetings, the research, and the policy work were overwhelming. I had bogged down keeping the record of Clinton's administration. After five years, I knew that I had to develop a new system, and I couldn't find the energy to do it. I told him. He looked down for a minute and told me that when I decided what I wanted to do he would help me make the change.

A couple of weeks later, a letter with some documents about a new apprenticeship program in Germany appeared on my desk. The governor asked me to look into it to see if such a program would work in this country. So I found myself intrigued again. I was used to Clinton asking me to look into programs in other states. His theory was that every problem had been solved somewhere, and he wanted to borrow other states' ideas and share our successes with others. Now he was looking beyond national borders for solutions. Hillary Clinton had discovered in Israel the Home Instruction Program for Preschool

Youngsters (HIPPY), the highly successful program for training parents to help their children be prepared for kindergarten, and she had imported it to Arkansas.

The new program cured my burnout. I became excited about it and also devised a new system for keeping Clinton's Arkansas record up-to-date.

I watched Bill Clinton grow into the presidency. He will be one of our greatest presidents, I believe. And he will still, figuratively and literally, eat apples all the way to the stem.

We Can't Park Here

MIKE GAULDIN

 **B**ill Clinton was more an idea than a person to me when I became his press secretary in 1987. I knew his record. I knew him through the newspapers and through the eyes of a mutual friend, Diane Blair, professor of political science at the University of Arkansas. I knew his failings well because I had often lampooned him during my days as an editorial cartoonist at the *Springdale News*. He knew me well enough to recognize me on the street and to talk about my cartoons. But since Bill Clinton knew nearly every other voter in Arkansas at least that well, I didn't claim to know him personally. I was by no means a true believer.

When I unexpectedly got the opportunity to work for him, I quickly saw myself working not for Bill Clinton, the man from Hope, Arkansas, but for Bill Clinton, the hope of Arkansas. He became to me an icon, a symbol, the hope of all Arkansans made flesh and given a voice. Bill Clinton possessed the will and the power, I thought, to make things better for my native state. If Arkansas has a chance to get off its knees in my lifetime, I reasoned, this is the politician who can come closest to making it happen.

I still saw him, though, as a cardboard cutout of a person, an ambitious politician who really had his eye on the United States Senate or even the White House, someone with whom I would never make, or even care to make, a personal connection. But I was willing to serve his ambition if I could do my part to help Arkansas.

This seemed to me to be a deceitful attitude for a press secretary to have, so I confessed it to him when I was called to the governor's mansion to meet him. I figured it would cost me the job.

"Will you stay with me for four years?" he asked.

"I will stick by you as long as you help Arkansas," I replied. "I know you're headed on to other things, and I can't promise you that I'll follow you out of state when that time comes. That's not where my interests are. But if you help Arkansas—as long as you help Arkansas—I'll stick with you no matter what."

Clinton said nothing but shot a quick glance across the living room to Betsey Wright, his chief of staff, and I knew that I had talked myself out of the job.

Three days later, Betsey telephoned and said that Bill Clinton wanted me to be his press secretary. That was the first time, but not the last, that Clinton confused the hell out of me.

• • •

When Bill Clinton appeared on the Johnny Carson show in 1988 after the never-ending speech at the Democratic National Convention, he talked about why he had decided a year before not to run for president, and he fell naturally into the standard answer that he had been giving for a year. The major reason that he had not run was that Chelsea was too young, only seven years old.

We waited a couple of hours until the show had aired in Arkansas, and then Clinton excitedly called Hillary and Chelsea to learn if they had liked the show.

When he got Chelsea on the telephone, he asked, "What'd you think, honey?"

She replied simply, "I'm eight."

• • •

During an informal session with the Capitol Press Corps in the late 1980s, Clinton was asked why he thought he was so well received by out-of-state members of the media and so harshly criticized by the press in Little Rock.

He smiled, shrugged, and cited the biblical observation, "A prophet is without honor in his own land."

After the session, he asked what I thought of his answer. I said, jokingly, "It was okay, but I think you offered the wrong quote. Shouldn't that be, 'a knight without armor in a savage land'?"

"No," he said, "that's the theme from 'Paladin.'"

"You mean, '"Have gun, will travel" reads the card of the man . . .'"

"Right," Clinton said, beginning to sing. "'A knight without armor in a savage land . . .' Don't ya'll remember that?" He turned to my assistants, Susie Whitacre and Trey Schroeder, who were standing off to the side, exchanging quizzical glances. Both were in their twenties and too young to have sat spellbound while Richard Boone tromped around the TV west in his dashing black outfit, whipping out that little derringer that he carried in his belt buckle.

"Sure," Clinton continued, "you must know that." And he sang: "'Have gun, will travel' reads the card of the man . . .'"

I joined in and, as Susie and Trey edged quietly toward the door, we performed an impromptu duet of the "Theme from Paladin."

The Rhodes scholar knew all the words and delivered them with perfect pitch. I think he was rather proud of it.

• • •

The first year that I worked for Clinton, he flew from Little Rock to Springdale to attend the annual gridiron show performed by northwest Arkansas journalists. I met him at the airport in Springdale, and he turned down the state police car provided for him and rode to the Arts Center of the Ozarks in my beat-up 1965 Volkswagen.

A very large parking space had been left for us in front of the theater, guarded by a stern "No Parking" sign. We were late, as usual, so I whipped in and began climbing out of the car.

"Wait," he said. "We can't park here, can we?"

"Governor," I said, "you're the governor, aren't you?"

"Oh, yeah," he said, as he clambered out. "I forgot."

Then We Serve

James L. "Skip" Rutherford

In the final days of the 1992 presidential campaign, Bill Clinton made a campaign stop on the campus of the University of Arkansas, where some eighteen years earlier, as a twenty-seven-year-old law professor, he had launched his political career by running against a popular Republican congressman.

Top campaign lieutenants argued that the stop in Fayetteville was a poor use of the candidate's scarce time. He was far ahead in Arkansas, but his presence at that eleventh hour might make a difference in a dozen toss-up states. However, several advisors, among them Senator David Pryor, Diane Blair, Craig Smith, and Susan Thomases (who was in charge of scheduling), thought Clinton needed an emotional uplift to carry him through the last grueling days before the election.

Supporters in Fayetteville provided the morale boost Clinton needed. Old friends greeted him at the airport. People carrying "welcome home" signs lined the roads into town, and thousands more covered the grounds in front of Old Main, where he spoke.

Afterward, I walked back into Old Main to browse among the rooms where I had attended classes more than twenty years earlier. The magnificent building had been shuttered for years but had recently been restored. A few minutes later, Clinton walked into the room where I was standing.

"Thank you," he said. "It was wonderful. Guess who I saw out there? I saw Myrna Martin, Pat Storey, and Rosemary Prewitt."

The large contingent of national press accompanying Clinton would not have recognized the names. Neither would many others outside of Washington County, because Myrna Martin, Pat Storey, and Rosemary Prewitt are not big names in Arkansas politics. They were, however, longtime friends and loyal supporters of Bill Clinton, and among the scores of influential people who turned out that night, they stood out to him. They had been with him since that first euphoric campaign, in 1974, when youthful friends gathered at the D-Lux, Herman's, and B&B Barbecue on the way out of town, but scheduling commitments and sheer logistics prevented it.

That night in Fayetteville I finally realized that my friend was going to be elected president of the United States. I stood in the spot where I had stood as a freshman in the autumn twenty-four years earlier; when the University of Arkansas band broke into the fight song, I was covered again with chill bumps, and this time the tears flowed.

I met Bill Clinton in 1974 at the home of Steve Smith in Fayetteville. Steve and I had been fraternity brothers and allies in campus politics, and I had worked in Steve's successful campaigns for the Arkansas House of Representatives, first when he was only twenty years old in 1970 and again in 1972. Later, Steve would become an administrative assistant to Clinton while he was attorney general and during his first term as governor.

Steve told me in 1974 that Clinton was "going places" in politics. I thought going places meant as governor or as a United States senator. I think Steve suspected more than that.

We were together in Washington when Bill took the oath of office. I couldn't keep my mind off Fayetteville. I remembered the visit in Steve's living room. I thought about Diane Blair, Bill's and Hillary's close friend, who is professor of political science at the university. I thought about Old Main and Myrna Martin, Pat Storey, and Rosemary Prewitt.

While we were leaving the Capitol, I ran into Michael Dukakis, the former governor of Massachusetts who was the 1988 Democratic presidential nominee. I introduced myself. He had just seen the governor of a small, rural southern state attain the job he himself had wanted so badly, but he was gracious and complimentary of both the new president and the campaign. He seemed stunned, though, when I told him that he had contributed significantly to the victory. Clinton had learned from Dukakis's defeat that a candidate could not merely disdain the dirty tricks of the Republicans—one had to fight back, also.

• • •

Clinton is known for his late-night telephone calls. He called one evening while I was dining at a friend's house. He had announced that day that his school reforms would include a mandatory basic-skills test for all teachers, and many teachers were outraged. He called several people, me among them, to gauge the reaction. I told him that he was right and that the public and many teachers would stand with him. School issues often brought our families together. Hillary founded the Home Instructional Program for Pre-School Youngsters (HIPPY), and we instituted it in the Little Rock schools.

Our daughters became friends and participated in the Hillcrest Softball League, a neighborhood league for girls. You learn a lot about people at the ballpark, and my best memories of the Clintons are from watching our daughters play. One season, Chelsea Clinton and our daughter, Martha Luin, were on the same team, the Molar Rollers, sponsored by a local dentist.

One spring evening I arrived after the game had begun. There had been a major world event, the specifics of which I have forgotten. I saw Bill standing behind the backstop screen, his fingers laced through the wire. I walked up to him and asked, "What do you think about what happened today?"

He looked at me and said, "Our defense is terrible."

"What?" I said.

"We're playing terrible defense."

I realized that he was focusing on the game and not the world. It was a little refreshing.

After the team had committed another error, he turned to me and said, "What are you doing this weekend?"

"I don't know," I said. "What's going on?"

"We need to practice," he said. "We can do it Saturday."

"We need to what?"

"Practice," he said. "We need practice."

"Bill, we're not the coaches," I said. "We can't call a practice."

Even at the ballpark, he was competitive. He knew the importance of practice.

Another time, I was sitting with Hillary in the stands and a little girl walked up to the plate carrying a bat bigger than she was. Her mother yelled out, "Come on, Susie, hit the ball."

Susie swung and missed. She then stepped back up to the plate. From the stands a familiar voice called out, "Come on, Susie, get a hit."

Without turning around, Susie recognized the voice. She walked out of the batter's box and looked up into the stands. Her little eyes were as big as saucers because the First Lady of Arkansas had cheered for her. I don't know Susie, but the look in her eyes acknowledged the thrill of having Hillary Rodham Clinton on her side and told a wonderful story.

Hillary usually throws out the first ball on opening day of the Hillcrest Softball League. However, the demands of the presidential campaign in 1992 gave people cause to believe that she wouldn't be able to do it that year. A week before the scheduled opening, I received a call from one of the Clinton advance people.

"Excuse me," she said. "But could you please tell me what is the Hillcrest Softball League? Mrs. Clinton is planning her schedule so that she can throw out the first ball."

On opening day, when Hillcrest's own Harry Caray, Jimmy Faulkner, introduced her, he said, "And next year, we'll have the Hillcrest Softball League opening-day ceremonies on the White House lawn." Don't rule it out.

It was at the ballpark in the spring of 1991 that I first thought Bill would run for president. Hillary and I were sitting in the bleachers, and she kept saying that it was important for someone to have the courage to carry a different message to the American people in 1992. The Democrats needed a message and a messenger, she said. I knew she must be saying that to Bill, too.

One morning that summer, I was jogging in our neighborhood when Craig Smith, a longtime Clinton staff member, drove alongside me. "The governor wants you to come to the mansion right now," he said.

"Right now?" I protested. "I haven't even brushed my teeth."

"Doesn't matter," Craig said. "Get in and let's go. He's only got an hour. He says it's important."

We gathered in the kitchen, Bill, Hillary, Craig, Bruce Lindsey, and me. For olfactory and sartorial reasons, I stayed on the opposite side of the room.

The topic was whether or not Bill Clinton should run for president. I thought it was a long shot at best but encouraged him to run, anyway. The pros and cons were discussed, and we talked at length about what would happen to Bill if he ran and lost.

"But, Governor," Bruce interjected, "what happens if we win?"

After a moment of silence, Hillary smiled, then spoke. "Then we serve."

On November 4, the morning after the election, I spoke with Bruce on the phone, and I repeated his prophetic question, "What happens if we win?"

"You know the worst thing about winning?" he asked. "You have to shave on Saturday."

Bill's presidential campaign began in an old paint store on West Seventh Street in Little Rock. On October 2, 1991, the day before Clinton's announcement, Bruce's wife, Bev, reminded us that we needed some music for the event. Bruce remembered that Bill had told him once that he liked the Fleetwood Mac song "Don't Stop Thinkin' about Tomorrow."

No one had a tape of the song. The campaign headquarters didn't even have a tape player. After several calls to record stores in Little

Rock, Bruce found a copy and drove out to pick it up. We all listened to it in the car of David Watkins, a friend from Hope who had played a key role in Bill's campaigns.

Not one member of the Arkansas congressional delegation could be present for Bill's announcement in front of the Old State House. Hillary asked me to draft a letter from the delegation to be read. I wrote the letter and received approval from Senators Dale Bumpers and David Pryor and from Representatives Bill Alexander, Ray Thornton, and Beryl Anthony to affix their names to it. I called Hillary at the mansion and read it to her. She asked me to read it at Bill's announcement.

It's still almost unbelievable that a person who honored a campaign commitment by returning to Bald Knob to attend a strawberry festival, a man who got sick while overachieving in the tomato-eating contest at the Pink Tomato Festival at Warren, and the person who danced with his wife on a downtown street of conservative Fort Smith because he had carried the county in the last gubernatorial election is now the most powerful person on the planet. In politics, as in softball, practice pays off.

Progressive Politics in Dogpatch*

ROY REED

Every time I go to town
The boys keep kicking my dog around.
I don't care if he is a hound,
They better quit kicking my dog around.

If Arkansas has a reputation beyond its borders (I recently encountered a waitress next door in Tennessee who could not locate Arkansas on the map), it is of a place inhabited by sullen, defensive rednecks who just want to be left alone with their hound dogs.

There is something to be said for such isolation, backwardness and all. However, the actual condition of Arkansas nowadays barely resembles its national reputation.

*A shorter version of this article appeared originally in *The New York Times Magazine*, September 6, 1992.

Contrary to some opinion, Bill Clinton is not a sport of nature thrown up from an abyss of ignorance, racism, and narrow-minded provincialism. Arkansas has plenty of those failings, but no more than most other states. The fact is, there is a strain of political progressivism here that goes far back into the state's history. That strain has dominated the state's politics for much of the time since the 1930s.

Some people in the North see only redneck Bubbas when they look south. That perception is not entirely the work of the social scholars who write for the big-city tabloids. The South has plenty of rednecks. And southerners have cultivated the redneck image to some extent to deceive outsiders into thinking that all of us down here are a bunch of country boys, easily gulled. Historically, that has meant that the outsider should keep one hand on his wallet. In my part of the South there is also a tendency not to care much about the world's good opinion. If New York's style is in-your-face, Arkansas's is mind-your-own-business. To our discomfort, we are now being asked to explain ourselves, thanks to Bill Clinton.

So, how do we explain a strain of progressive politics in this dogpatch of a place? There are several causes. Alongside a lot of bad luck, poverty, mismanagement, corruption, and violence stretching back to the nineteenth century, Arkansas has been fortunate in certain of its leaders and institutions. It had a strong but little-known cadre of activist women that predated today's feminism. It was blessed, until 1991, with a statewide newspaper of uncommon elegance and influence. The same poverty that has dogged the state from its beginning has spawned a hardy political reaction that has tended continuously, if erratically, toward anti-establishment populism, throwing up a succession of leaders who have tried to stand up for common people.

It might surprise some outsiders to learn that Bill Clinton, the Democratic centrist, started his political life as a populist liberal. I covered his first race for public office in 1974, an unsuccessful campaign for Congress, and was astonished to hear this twenty-eight-year-old law-school teacher addressing conservative Rotary clubs on the dangers of corporate abuse of power. Beware of the multinational corporations, he said. The Rotarians applauded. He had recently immersed himself in the 1972 presidential campaign of George McGovern, and was proud to call himself a liberal. Clinton hushed some of his advanced rhetoric after he entered statewide politics, but there is no evidence that he abandoned his populism. Echoes of it could be heard in his campaign speeches in 1992 as he lashed out at the powerful few at the top of the economic ladder.

The progressive-populist strain is not hard to trace in Arkansas. The state has had more than its share of political plunderers, and the ordinary people have had to fight back hard.

With a few noble exceptions, the state's founders in the 1830s were a band of thieves. They stole land, money, and resources impartially from their fellow European settlers and the resident Quapaws. ("Arkansas" is a tortured rendering, through French and Indian tongues, of Quapaw, which means Downstream People.) Shortly after Arkansas gained statehood in 1836, banking and bond scandals erupted that ruined Arkansas's reputation for generations. The first session of the legislature in 1837 was distinguished chiefly for a murder: the House speaker stabbed a colleague with a Bowie knife, one of the state's first manufactured products.

The state's most famous jurist to this day is the late Isaac C. Parker, a federal judge who hanged murderers up to six at a time on the Oklahoma border and never got the job finished. Desperadoes ruled the countryside without much interference from state authority during much of the nineteenth century. During Reconstruction, Arkansas had its own little civil war that included at least four political assassinations and an outbreak of gunfire for control of the capitol.

Understandably, a suspicion of politicians was one of the earliest attributes of the Arkansas mentality. John Gould Fletcher, poet and a historian of his state, said it remained strong into the twentieth century, especially in the hill man. "He warn't getting nowheres, with most of the land worthless and the rest of it wearing out. Them politician fellers in Little Rock, the high-stovepipe-hat, silk-stocking crowd, had never done a danged thing for him or his kind." Echoes of that sentiment can still be heard in the hills and small towns, and even in the cotton-socks wards of Little Rock.

All the while, there was fermenting in the state a political spirit that bordered on revolutionary. The populist movement that swept the

South and part of the West during the last years of the 1800s had one of its strongest branches in rural Arkansas. Farmers here had a hard time deciding whom they hated most, the bandits on Wall Street or the bankers on Main Street. A turn-of-the-century governor named Jeff Davis inherited the populist mantle and ran all his political races against Wall Street and "those high-collared roosters" in Little Rock. (Davis eventually went to the Senate. At one of his first fancy dinners in Washington, seated between two ladies, he took a bite of something hot and promptly spit it onto the floor. In the hush that followed, he said to his shocked table mates, "Some damn fools would have swallowed that.")

Populism was not strong enough for some Arkansawyers, as the residents called themselves until a few years ago when, in a fit of image improvement, an unsettling number became Arkansans. A few thousand took up a kind of barnyard Marxism and voted Socialist between 1900 and World War I. In 1910, an Ozarks farmer named Sam Faubus named his oldest child Orval Eugene after his hero Eugene V. Debs. Then he organized the Greasy Creek chapter of the Socialist party and signed up almost every family in the neighborhood. The boy grew up to become Arkansas's most famous governor until Bill Clinton came along. Faubus was the one who challenged the federal courts on school desegregation in 1957 and forced President Eisenhower to send federal troops to Little Rock to put black children into Central High School.

During the Depression, Arkansas's progressive strain was effective enough to help President Roosevelt enact the New Deal. The Senate Majority Leader was Joseph T. Robinson of Arkansas, who had been Al Smith's running mate in the unsuccessful Democratic campaign of 1928. Senator Robinson steered FDR's legislation through the Senate. Back home in Arkansas, he also fought the Ku Klux Klan.

In 1932, the year Franklin D. Roosevelt defeated President Herbert Hoover, the voters of Arkansas made progressive history in another way. They elected Hattie W. Caraway to the United States Senate. She was the first woman elected to a full term in that body.

During that same period, a campaign against lynching was launched all across the South. The leaders were unlikely heroes—

high-born and well-to-do white women. Arkansas had an outspoken group led by Adolphine Terry, sister of the poet Fletcher and wife of a U.S. congressman, David D. Terry. Mrs. Terry had been educated at Vassar. She and her friends threw themselves into the campaign vigorously, and, aided by the *Arkansas Gazette,* effectively put a stop to the barbarism in Arkansas. The sympathy that the women developed for black people during those years carried over into another fight a generation later. When Little Rock was thrust into the world spotlight in the struggle to desegregate its schools, Mrs. Terry and her "ladies"—many now young enough to be her daughters or granddaughters—turned the tide in favor of racial justice.

The progressive impulse continued in the late 1930s. Governor Carl Bailey bucked the political establishment—dominated by delta planters, some of whom kept their workers in a state of near-peonage—by advocating social welfare for the poor, elderly, and disabled. He reorganized the state welfare department to qualify Arkansas for full participation in all federal welfare programs. But perhaps his main contribution was to help elect to the Senate a bright young man named J. William Fulbright, who was running against an enemy of Bailey. Homer M. Adkins had defeated Bailey for governor in 1940. Bailey took his revenge four years later by campaigning for Fulbright against Adkins for the Senate.

As a freshman congressman, Fulbright had already passed the resolution that led directly to the formation of the United Nations after World War II. He went on in the Senate to become a leader in disarmament and international education, and in the 1960s he became the main congressional critic of the Vietnam War.

Fulbright will be remembered for one other accomplishment: He exposed young Bill Clinton to national politics and became his first political mentor.

Lee Williams, Senator Fulbright's administrative assistant, was looking for someone to help around the office in 1968. Bill Clinton had been recommended by an Arkansas political ally who had seen the youngster at work in a state campaign earlier. Williams telephoned Clinton in Arkansas. He said, "You can have a part-time job for $3,500 a year or a full-time job for $5,000." Clinton asked, "How about two part-time jobs?" Williams said, "You're just the guy I'm looking for. Be here Monday."

On the Fulbright staff, the young man did whatever needed doing. Among other things, he helped set up public hearings on the Vietnam War. He watched and listened as Senator Fulbright, chairman of the Foreign Relations Committee, grilled the generals and cabinet officers and aroused the nation's conscience over America's involvement in Southeast Asia. He also noticed Fulbright's obsession with education. When he himself became a Rhodes scholar, it was a matter of pride to him that his hero had been one, too.

Williams said recently, "There's no doubt that Fulbright was a major influence on Clinton." Big events were taking place, and the young man soaked them up "like a sponge"—all the while studying the Fulbright style and character.

Clinton was not the only Arkansas politician influenced by Senator Fulbright. Among the others was David H. Pryor, now a senator, who went to Washington as a Senate page when he was a boy and was struck with admiration for Arkansas's distinguished senator. Even Dale Bumpers, the man who defeated Fulbright in 1974, was one of his admirers. Scores, perhaps hundreds, of progressive political activists in Arkansas trace their interest in public affairs to the Fulbright example.

And Fulbright was not the only role model. Arkansas for a long time has been particular about the men and women it sent to Washington. Two of Fulbright's colleagues in Congress became national stars and, each in his own way, a champion of progressivism.

Brooks Hays, a silver-tongued country lawyer, entered the House of Representatives after a lengthy career in local and state politics. He was a favorite of his fellows in the House, partly because of his humor—he was a world-class storyteller—but mainly because he took his religious precepts seriously. When the desegregation crisis erupted at Central High, Hays intervened to bring the federal and state camps together. His reconciliation effort cost him his seat in Congress in 1958. The voters decided, correctly, that he was an integrationist. In those days, integration was thought to be a form of Communism.

Wilbur Mills, for most of his congressional career, was known as one of the most influential men in Washington. A generation of newspaper readers grew up thinking that the word powerful was part of his title—as "Wilbur Mills, chairman of the powerful Ways and Means Committee . . ." His knowledge of the tax code and his quiet use of power tended to obscure a record of progressive achievement. It is largely forgotten by the public that his most impressive accomplishment was not the drunken seduction of a strip-tease dancer but the shaping of a legislative package that became Medicare.

• • •

Race was the all-determining, crippling issue in the South from the beginning of the nation until the 1960s. But in Arkansas, out on the western edge of the region, up against the Indian Territory, race was never the whole political story. The state had its vicious moments: The Elaine riots in eastern Arkansas in 1919, in which five whites and between twenty-five and two hundred blacks were killed in a frenzy of race hatred; violent reaction by planters to the efforts of black and white sharecroppers to form a union in the 1930s; the ugly mobs at Central High School in the late 1950s. But throughout modern times, white Arkansawyers have generally been more accommodating toward their black neighbors than have the white people of the Deep South. That has been reflected, however imperfectly, in the state's politics.

Sidney S. McMath, a war hero, came home and took over the governor's office in 1948. He was a friend of President Harry S. Truman and a national Democrat all the way—even on the race issue.

One of McMath's protégés was another World War II veteran, Orval Faubus. When Faubus took his turn as governor, he started in the same liberal vein. He appointed the first black members of the state Democratic Central Committee. He watched, and did not obstruct, the desegregation of several school districts around the state after the 1954 Supreme Court decision decreeing an end to segregated public schools. Then his opponents began to attack him as an integrationist, the one label that no southern politician could afford in the 1950s. He finally gave in to massive segregationist pressure and made his play against the federal courts in 1957. That won him four more terms—six altogether—and an indelible stigma in the national mind.

It also tarnished what was in many ways an unusually progressive record. He raised taxes for education and other services. He reformed the snake pit of a state mental hospital into a modern institution. He built the state's first facility for retarded youngsters. He became close to the rich men who held behind-the-scenes power, but he also kept friendly ties to union labor. He built new bridges to the black community after the anger of 1957 subsided, and even brought in some of his former black enemies as advisors.

Governor Faubus had a role in electoral reform when a modern voter-registration system replaced the poll tax in 1964. His legislative advisor helped draft the new voter-registration law, then joined the League of Women Voters to get it passed in a statewide election. Voting machines and clean elections replaced the poll tax and political-machine fraud, at least in the more populous counties.

Some of the old bosses got on the bandwagon. The day after the election, the governor's legislative advisor and a friend were having lunch in downtown Little Rock when the political boss of one of the delta counties stopped at their table. He and his cronies had been swayed by the Faubus man's role in the reform effort. "I tell you what we did for you," he said. "We gave you an extra thousand votes and passed that son of a bitch."

Southerners have come to expect scorn from the rest of the country. They suspect that the scorn is tied somehow to the way they talk. To a southerner, a New York accent is strange, funny, exotic, or at worst a signal of approaching danger. To a New Yorker, a southern accent is mushmouth, grating, irritating, or at worst contemptible. Those are not matching perceptions. Both are grounded in regional prejudice, but one is more pernicious in the same way that white racism, coming from the dominant culture, is more pernicious than black racism. Many southerners believed that Bill Clinton's largest political problem was neither his politics nor his "character," but a pervasive regional scorn that wounds all of us down here, year in and year out.

Arkansawyers have probably been more image-conscious than most Americans, even most southerners, simply because their image has been so consistently poor. It is hard to say how much of the image of redneck benightedness is earned and how much is the result of a national need to poke fun at someone. Bob Lancaster, in his book *The Jungles of Arkansas,* devotes four pages to tracing the national myth that Arkansawyers don't wear shoes.

While mind-your-own-business is the main element of the Arkansas political style, there is also a quality that can only be called behind-your-back. The state has a tendency to allow important decisions to be made by important men in the quiet of their clubs and offices. In the last two generations, none have been more important than the men in and around the investment house of Stephens, Inc. The state has other wealthy businessmen, such as Don Tyson, whose family runs the largest poultry business in the world. The heirs of the late Sam Walton of Bentonville still own the nation's largest fortune. But none have been so influential in Arkansas politics as the brothers W. R. (Witt) and Jackson T. Stephens.

Before Witt died in 1991, he had been the most important king-maker in Arkansas politics since the 1940s. He grew wealthy in bonds, investments, and natural gas. He used his money, and that of his friends, to shape policy in Little Rock and in Washington. He was politically friendly with all but two of the first ten Arkansas governors after World War II. One of those two was Winthrop Rockefeller, who didn't need Stephens' money. The other was Dale Bumpers, now a senator, who simply did not like the Stephenses. Of the remaining eight, Bill Clinton probably had less to do with the Stephenses than any of the others. He maintained a kind of strained cordiality, but without much trust on either side.

Arkansas's big men have had a lot of attention in the press, but they do not always get their way. Witt Stephens was not able to beat or join Dale Bumpers. The state's richest citizens formed an organization, nicknamed the Good Suit Club, to upgrade higher education. They quietly let it drop after running into opposition in the legislature.

Clinton's support was always so broad based that he did not have to rely heavily on any one person or special interest. That is not to say that he was unfriendly to special interests; it is just that no one small band of interests controlled him. With the death of Witt Stephens, the state no longer had any behind-the-scenes giant. Even he had lost much of his dominance long before he died.

Diane Blair, a political scientist at the University of Arkansas and the author of *Arkansas Politics and Government,* argues that Arkansas never has had as large or as powerful an elite as the older states of the Confederacy. She notes that although slaves were essential to the cotton economy here, as elsewhere, Arkansas never had many big slave owners. Populism was always more vital here than in some other states. The large planters managed to throw their weight around, but there were always the mule-headed hill people who went their own way.

Sometime during the 1950s and 1960s, as blacks left the plantations and voting was regularized, and as the rest of the state prospered and asserted itself, the planters became just another interest group. The old, small rural elite gave way to a business elite in the cities, triggering a demand for a more presentable class of politicians: people like Bill Fulbright, a university president; Sid McMath, a modern, educated man; David Pryor, a polished reformer; Winthrop Rockefeller, a transplanted sophisticate from New York; Dale Bumpers, a successful lawyer; and Bill Clinton, Oxford, Yale, Georgetown—a politician who would never spit his food on the floor, no matter what the provocation.

These moderate, presentable politicians, like their predecessors going back to the 1930s, have been elected by a coalition of urban and small-town voters who have increasingly demanded clean government and some semblance of progressive ideas. Since the abolition of the poll tax, African Americans, who make up about 16 percent of the population, have tended to vote overwhelmingly for these New South officeholders.

How a voting majority developed a taste for progressive politics is hard to explain. Professor Blair grapples with the question for several pages, suggesting several theories. One that has credibility among many observers is the longtime progressive influence of the *Arkansas Gazette,* which died in 1991 after 172 years of publication. (Actually, the paper was assassinated by a mindless national corporation of the kind that Arkansawyers have historically despised.) David Pryor once said, "The major difference between Arkansas and the rest of the South has been the *Arkansas Gazette.*"

The *Gazette* opposed lynching when it was unpopular to do so. It opposed the Arkansas Power and Light Company, the dominant political influence during the 1930s and 1940s, because the *Gazette*'s owner thought no one interest should exercise so much power. It opposed Governor Faubus over his school desegregation actions in 1957 and lost thirty thousand subscribers in a month. From the 1950s on, it favored almost every liberal position on its editorial page. Even people who hated its editorials read it because it was literate and filled with information they needed. Unlike some Deep South states, Arkansas had this provocative counterweight to the conservative inclination, and it made a difference. Those who grieve its passing wonder how long its influence will survive its death, and whether the remaining statewide newspaper, the *Arkansas Democrat-Gazette,* will be able to fill the gap.

But deeper than the influence of any one institution has been the phenomenon of populism, born of poverty and hard times, married at some point to middle-class progressivism.

Arkansas from the beginning has ranked at or near the bottom in virtually all of the national indices of economic well-being. The state now ranks forty-seventh in per-capita income, up marginally from dead last when I was a boy. Although there is evidence that the past year has seen Arkansas's personal income growth outpace the nation's, census figures for the 1980s show that the state's median household income dropped from 73 percent of the national median to 70 percent at the end of the decade. Lagging behind the rest of the country has inspired generations of populist resentment against big wealth and its political influence.

Alongside that resentment there has been a long, continuing reaction against corrupt politics and electoral fraud. The latest scholarship on Arkansas politics is *How I Stole Elections,* by Marlin Hawkins, a former sheriff of Conway County up the Arkansas River from Little Rock. Sheriff Hawkins had the last perfectly running political machine in the state. In his prime, he could deliver votes for a chosen candidate to within one hundred of the exact number needed to win. The retired boss has become a folk hero, partly because everyone understands that his kind of politics, colorful and entertaining as it was, has been replaced by a more punctilious type. The clean-government crowd, especially in the towns and cities, has provided the spark for much of the progressivism in Arkansas during recent years. The voters who came of age during the decline of machine politics seem to prefer not only cleaner government, but also more forward-looking policies. For example, no serious candidate for office would now think of alienating the black electorate. Candidates routinely portray themselves as champions of equal rights and social welfare.

A darkening corridor of the Arkansas State Capitol reveals opposing bronze busts of the two men who were, until recently, the state's most important governors. Their sculptors have put an impish grin on Orval Faubus and a grim face on Winthrop Rockefeller—masks of comedy and tragedy almost the reverse of the real-life personas of the two men. In a way, those two busts encapsulate the entire contradictory history of Arkansas politics.

Faubus was probably the last American political figure to have been born in a log cabin. He grew up not only in a socialist household but also in what today would be called poverty. He knew both hard work and hardship. Rockefeller was reared in a wealthy Republican nest in New York. His grandfather was the man who cornered the market in kerosene, among other things, and raised the price so high that families like the Faubuses could barely afford it. Winthrop spent his playboy years squandering the fruits of that greed.

But when Rockefeller succeeded Faubus, who retired as governor in 1966, he carved a reputation as the great reformer and modernizer of Arkansas politics. It was Rockefeller's money that financed the difficult work of putting 105,000 black voters on the Arkansas registration lists after the abolition of the poll tax in 1964. He forced the old machine politicians to accommodate themselves to a new reality in Arkansas. Hundreds of thousands of voters not only came to expect clean politics but also gained a new respect for racial tolerance and social welfare.

Since the Rockefeller era, virtually all of the state's governors, senators, and representatives have been considered progressive, sometimes even (hated word) liberal. Senators Bumpers and Pryor have found themselves uncomfortably often in the company of northern liberals when those annual rankings of voting records are published. In 1992 a thirty-one-year-old woman named Blanche Lambert upset a twelve-term congressman, Bill Alexander, in the Democratic primary and easily won election in November. She is from an old planter family of the delta. Amazingly, she is an unabashed liberal.

When Bill Clinton toured the country advocating health-care reform, taxing the rich, increased spending for education and job creation, and, in the old populist tradition, throwing the big-money rascals out, he was in no danger of alienating his home constituency. Indeed, this small piece of middle America may now be as eager to move into the twenty-first century as any other place in the country, if only to put on speed in escaping the past.

Big Wheels
Keep on Turnin'

GEORGE FISHER

Reprinted with permission, *Arkansas Democrat-Gazette*

**News Item: Governor Clinton wishes to be
removed from Cartoonist's baby buggy.**

Reprinted with permission, *Arkansas Democrat-Gazette*

Reprinted with permission, *Arkansas Democrat-Gazette*

Reprinted with permission, *Arkansas Democrat-Gazette*

Reprinted with permission, *Arkansas Democrat-Gazette*

Reprinted with permission, *Arkansas Democrat-Gazette*

Reprinted with permission, *Arkansas Democrat-Gazette*

Afterword

This compendium of recollections from those who have known the Clintons well was not meant to be inclusive. It might have been expanded a thousandfold and not embraced all who felt they had unique insights into the character of the Clintons, a special understanding of their graces and faults, each arrived at, if not by long friendship, at least by a fleeting but nonetheless deeply personal bond. People in Arkansas took personally each of Bill Clinton's victories, compromises, and failures, as they might have looked upon the misfortunes and glories of a promising but chronically errant nephew. For a generation, analyzing the Clintons' comings and goings was by far the most common subject of political discussion in Arkansas.

As these essays suggest, Bill Clinton has always sought friendship and approval on a widening scale. Who expects otherwise of a good politician? But the impulse seems to be at least as intrinsic to Clinton's nature as it is political. At times he seems to imagine a mystical tether with people on a vast scale, which he must keep in good repair by talking to them on the most personal level he can find. This did not change when he ascended to the presidency. He still goes out and talks to people and, to the extent that this is limited by the constraints of the office, carries on through the airwaves an extended personal dialogue, an electronic friendship, with each of them. You know me, he seems to say, and together we will all run the country. It is a risky notion of governing, but one not as yet discredited by Bill and Hillary Clinton. Perhaps never to be.

Ernest Dumas